A CUP OF SUGAR, NEIGHBOR

By
JEANETTE LOCKERBIE

D1115851

MOODY PRESS
CHICAGO

23 25 27 29 30 28 26 24

Printed in the United States of America

FOR
Babe,
my sister-in-law,
and
loving "good neighbor"

A CUP OF SUGAR, NEIGHBOR

BIBLE READING: 2 Kings 4:1-6

Borrow from your neighbors and friends (v. 3).

There was a time when neighbors "neighbored" more than we do today. And frequently, the borrowing of a cup of sugar or some other commodity had a lot to do with it. There were practical reasons for this neighborly cooperation: no supermarkets with their loaded shelves tempted the shopper to stock up; the corner store may have been much farther than "the corner"; and with two and three-car families practically unknown, transportation was a problem for the homemaker.

So, when a woman ran short, she just walked over to her neighbor's house and borrowed. Invariably this led to friendly visiting so that sometimes the actual reason for coming was less important than the neighborliness it engendered.

Not having such reasonable excuses for borrowing, we have substituted the coffee klatch as a means of togetherness. For, even in our space age with its plethora of technical diversions, the need for sociability is as great as it ever was, perhaps greater. But sometimes, even today, we do borrow a cup of sugar.

The classic instance of one woman's borrowing from another is in the Bible. An unnamed widow of one of Elisha's students borrowed at the command of the prophet. Her neighbors could not know that they were to be part of a miracle, that they would be included wherever the "widow's oil" story would be told. Suppose they had refused her request, had turned away from their door this needy woman!

We can't know what form human need will take as it knocks at our door today: perhaps a grieving widow, perhaps a neighbor with a hunger in her heart, not in her cupboard. That emptiness Christ is waiting to fill. Like the good neighbors of this "certain woman" in Bible times, you and I can sometimes have a part in a miracle.

And it won't cost us even a cup of sugar.

WHAT IT'S ALL ABOUT

BIBLE READING: Matthew 22:34-40

Keep only these and you will find you are obeying all the others (v. 40b, TLB*).

A new Christian asked a Bible teacher what the Bible is all about. His reply was, "It's about two things: our relationship with God and our relationship with one another."

Some people describe this as "our vertical and our horizontal relationships." (I always get confused as to which is which.)

The Lord Jesus put great emphasis on the importance of these two areas: loving the Lord our God and loving our neighbor. Sometimes I wonder if Jesus knew we would have greater difficulty with the second command than with the first. Loving our neighbor is a more "nuts and bolts," "cup of borrowed sugar" kind of strain. Loving God appears to be more abstract and, therefore, less practical and demanding, less tied into our daily routine.

But is it? Should it be? Or is loving God in fact the very wellspring from which comes our love for our neighbor, for one another? Jesus would not have said that loving God is the first and greatest commandment if it *were not*. Certainly God does not need our love to make Him feel complete (although He wants us to love Him). So the benefit must be for us when we love God. Isn't it as we wholeheartedly love the Lord our God that His love is then shed abroad in our hearts, and we have enough for ourselves and to spare—enough to share with our neighbors?

The Living Bible.

So, let's put first things first today, shall we? And we'll find that the other things will fall into place.

FORMULA FOR FAITHFULNESS

BIBLE READING: 1 Corinthians 4:1-5

Then shall every man have praise of God (v. 5b).

Have you ever thought what our world would be like if God had seen fit to populate it with just "stars"—only brilliant, outstanding people?

God uses all kinds of people; and as Abraham Lincoln is quoted as saying, "The good Lord must have loved the common people; He made so many of them."

Even as Christians we are prone to be impressed by those Christians who serve God in the limelight. But, at the same time, common sense tells us that, in every area of life, the people who keep the wheels oiled and running are ordinary mortals like you and me. This is true in the home; it's equally true in the church. Without the seemingly run-of-the-mill individuals, things would undoubtedly grind to a halt.

Not too many would recognize the name Bill Winslow; but in the lumber camps and isolated areas of Canada's northland, this was the man who, year after year, was practically the sole influence for God, the man who cared for the souls of men otherwise spiritually neglected. It was from this humble, home missionary I learned a great four-line lesson—a formula for faithfulness:

> Just praise the Lord for all that's passed,
> And pray that He will hold thee fast;
> And peg away while life shall last—
> Just praise—and pray—and peg away.

Praising and thanking God is a great tonic for our spirits, whatever our circumstances. It keeps us enthusiastic in our witness for Him.

Prayer is our vital link with God. Through it, we sense our partnership with Him in the greatest business in the world, however big or small our part may seem.

Peg away. Praise and prayer make it possible to persistently "peg away." It would be unthinkable that we could consistently praise God, commune with Him in prayer—and be a quitter.

Think what God can do with a whole host of Christians who live by this formula! Think what He can do with you and me!

THINK BIG

BIBLE READING: Ephesians 2:4-10

[God] has lifted us up from the grave into glory
(v. 6a, TLB).

As I slowed for a traffic light, a huge billboard caught my attention. "Think Big," it screamed. "Think Number One."

My mind translated the giant letters into Number One: *myself*, and I thought, *How self-centered can you be?*

But, dwelling on the idea the next couple of miles, I thought of something else. It was this: I can "think big" about myself, and it can be quite in order.

Care to try it with me?

What is the biggest thought that can enter your mind (and mine)? That we *belong to the Lord*. That God *so* loved us He gave heaven's best to reconcile us to Himself. That Jesus cared enough to come all the way from the ivory palaces to show us what God is like and then to die for us.

That He is preparing an eternal home for us and will one day come to take us to be with Him.

Can you think of anything more mind-boggling, more life-changing!

If you are like most of us, you become disheartened at times and begin to dwell on such thoughts as these: *I'm just a nobody; nobody cares what happens to me; nobody thinks I'm important.* Or you have some other self-belittling things.

That is the time when the message of the billboard takes on meaning. Even more, that is the time to look away above the highest billboard, look away to Jesus. We are His workmanship. He is responsible for us, and He has promised to love us, to care for us, and never to leave us. Have you ever thought that God does not create "nothing people"? Jesus did not die for "nobodies."

While we are exhorted not to think of ourselves more highly than we ought (Romans 12:3a), this does not give us license to downgrade ourselves, for we are Christ's workmanship, His redeemed property, because we have accepted Jesus as our Saviour.

Isn't that reason enough to think big about ourselves?

COPING WITH AIR FLIGHT FEARS

BIBLE READING: Psalm 139:7-12; Deuteronomy 33:27

Even there, . . . thy right hand shall hold me (v. 10).

Joan couldn't bring herself to take a plane trip. Even the thought of it made her shiver. For years she was able to avoid flying, but one day an emergency left her with no alternative.

Later, a friend said to her, "How did you ever manage to step aboard that plane? I know how petrified you must have been."

With a warm smile Joan explained, "Well, there I was, my heart in my mouth, just dreading the trip on that giant 747. I was telling a woman standing near me how I felt; and, just as our flight was called, she fished in her handbag and dug something out and pressed it into my hand. 'That's what always helps me,' she said, with a confident look."

"My! Whatever was it, Joan?" her friend was eager to know. "A tranquilizer?"

Joan thought for a moment then said, "In a way, yes, you could call it that. Here's what it was." She showed her friend a little two-inch-by-three-inch card. Together they read the words typed on it: *"The eternal God is thy refuge, and underneath are the everlasting arms"* (Deuteronomy 33:27).

"I had read that verse many times," Joan admitted. "I'd memorized it even, but it took that stranger's act of caring enough to share it with me to give it the meaning God meant it to have for me. I can honestly say that I latched onto this promise, and God wonderfully calmed my fears. When I felt myself getting tense and scared, I just said over and over, 'underneath are the everlasting arms, so why *should* I be so fearful?'"

Underneath? Underneath what? Underneath wherever we are, God is there.

When we appropriate this comfort for ourselves—this knowledge that we can never go high enough or low enough that God cannot reach out to help us—when this becomes a practical, "present help in trouble," we can share it with other people who need it and help calm their fears.

HELP THY NEIGHBOR

BIBLE READING: Hebrews 9:19-22; 1 John 1:7

Without shedding of blood is no remission (v. 22*b*).

A much-talked-about program on a Los Angeles television channel is "Help Thy Neighbor." It's a live audience format and offers opportunity for persons with special needs to air them and, hopefully, to receive help.

Not always are the people speaking for themselves; and, the time I viewed it, a man was appealing for blood for a relative suffering from leukemia. Massive quantities were needed. The response was tremendous; and, as the station's switchboard lit up with the incoming calls, the host of the program gave precise instructions to the donors.

"Be sure to give the *name* of the person for whom you are donating your blood, and the *name and address of the hospital* where she is a patient." He carefully spelled out and repeated this information. "We have to be sure you do this," he cautioned, "because blood is always in short supply and this is the only way we can be sure the blood is credited to the right person."

How often we hear the word *remission* in connection with leukemia.

As I listened to this program, the wonderful truth came to my mind. Christ has provided complete remission from the fatal sickness of sin. I thought, too, that the blood of Jesus Christ, God's Son, is never in short supply. And, certainly, it will never be in danger of being credited to the wrong person. Jesus shed His blood for "whosoever," but only those who admit to having the disease of sin and make application for this "blood donation" will ever have it credited to them. And "the Lord knoweth them that are his" (2 Timothy 2:19).

God has His "blood bank," and we can best help our

11

neighbors by introducing them to our Saviour, the Lord Jesus Christ. His blood matches every type on earth, and "Whosoever believeth in Him shall receive remission of sins" (Acts 10:43).

WHAT'S YOUR REASON?

BIBLE READING: 1 Peter 3:12-15; Psalm 42:11

Hope thou in God (Psalm 42:11).

Crisis situations tend to bring out what has been hidden in people's minds. Living as I do in "earthquake country," I recall a morning when we had been literally "all shook up" as the earth rumbled beneath us and objects around us began to do strange things.

Living in our area was a man whom his neighbors jestingly called "John the Baptist." But, as we gathered in little groups to assess our feelings and the damage to our property, more than one person said, "I wouldn't have minded being in 'John the Baptist's' shoes when the quake hit." A woman expressed herself this way: "I'm not a church-goer like Old John, but *I'm going to give my granddaughter a dollar for the collection plate on Sunday.*"

In their own way these people were voicing their lack of security and their new awareness of their need for it. They had recognized that their neighbor, John, possessed it. Now, by any means, they were eager to latch on to some contact with the living God whom they didn't seem to need in calmer times. The trouble with this was that their hope was wrongly based.

In fact, it is not enough to have hope. We have to have a *reason* for that hope, as the Bible tells us. And, as believers, we have the most solid of all reasons: our hope is *in God,* in the promise in His Word, in Jesus Christ Himself. As Paul writes it for us, "I know whom I have believed, and am persuaded that he is able to keep [me]" (2 Timothy 1:12).

When our world is rocking, whether by natural disaster or through personal crisis and tragedy, it is wonderful to be assured that we are on the solid rock, Christ Jesus.

It's good to take our "reason for hope" out and reevaluate it from time to time, to define it precisely for ourselves against the day of storm. (There will be no time then to begin asking, "In what am I *really* placing my trust?")

Once the matter of our reason for hope is settled, we can confidently share this hope with others so that they, too, may have a shelter in the time of storm.

THEY COME IN ALL SIZES

BIBLE READING: 1 Corinthians 13:1-4; Mark 10:13-14

Charity suffereth long, and is kind (v. 4a).

In the grocery check-out line, one woman said to another, "And speaking of neighbors, I have no complaint. I have good neighbors. But their *children!*" There was a world of dislike, of impatience, in her voice.

That set me thinking.

Do you suppose that, when Jesus gave His directive concerning loving our neighbor, He meant us to confine this love to adult neighbors only? I hardly think so. Nevertheless, maybe some of us can see ourselves in that woman in the grocery store. We're willing to show some understanding, to put up with certain attitudes of our neighbors, to make allowances for things they do which may not please us.

But this tolerance applies only to our adult neighbors. We don't tend to think of neighbors as coming in all sizes: small children, live-wire juniors, "difficult" teenagers, as well as adult men and women. So we rob ourselves as well as our youthful neighbors. How shortsighted can we be?

Children and young people respond to warmth and genuine interest. It is worth keeping in mind that, by our love and patience and kindness, we can greatly influence pliable young minds.

When we turn off a neighbor's child because his actions bother us, who knows if we might ultimately be at least partially responsible for his refusal to turn to the Lord— especially if this young person knows we profess to love the Lord? Can we afford to be this kind of Christian?

Little neighbors grow up to be big neighbors, and how wonderful if, by our love and demonstrated interest, we can be God's instruments to bring them into His kingdom! They will, in turn, realize that neighbors come in all sizes.

BALANCING OUR PRIORITIES

BIBLE READING: Luke 4:37-40; Titus 2:7

Sometimes as Christians we are so busy "serving the Lord" that we fail to respond as we are able to human need around us. It's not difficult to fall into such a pattern, to be somewhat unbalanced in our priorities.

"Love my neighbor!" exclaimed a Christian living in a large city, "I don't even *know* my neighbor," and she's not alone in this.

One experience along this line will always haunt me.

I had unlocked my apartment door and stepped out into the hall, ready to leave for my office. And there was a neighbor—just waiting for me. In near despair she poured out her tragic story. "I can't *stand* it," she said during her storm of tears. "Pray for me. Pray for me!" And she literally threw herself into my arms.

I listened. I did pray, and we wept together. In the ensuing days, I continued to pray and to show my concern for this neighbor. But as I left her that morning, somewhat calmed after my prayer, the thought in my own mind was, *What kind of a neighbor must she think I am, that she couldn't feel free to wake me up at any hour of the night to share her burden?* I know totally non-Christian women who are available to help other people at any time!

It is written concerning our Lord that He went about doing good (Acts 10:38). Doing good was a way of life with Him. He was available. He could be—and was—interrupted and disturbed by needy persons. Jesus was, first, last, and always "about His Father's business": eternal business, balanced by human need for Him to be a "present help" in their time of trouble. In this, He set us an example that in all things we should show ourselves a pattern of good works.

By balancing our own priorities, we can refute the criticism that "Some Christians are more concerned with 'souls' than with *people*."

NATIVE WISDOM

BIBLE READING: Psalm 19

Making wise the simple (v. 7b).

As far as anyone in town was aware, "Aunt Mary" had never attended college or university. But she so often had amazingly right answers that both young and older people came to her with their problems.

Perhaps you know such Christian people. They appear to have insight beyond other people in similar circumstances and with the same educational background. This should not surprise us. It was no secret to David, the psalmist: "I have more understanding than my teachers," he wrote, "for thy testimonies are my meditation" (Psalm 119:99).

And "the testimonies of the Lord are sure, making wise the simple," we read in Psalm 19.

"Native wisdom" we sometimes hear this called: a strange, unexplainable knowledge which cannot be accounted for by the individual's known educational advantages. But it is nevertheless unquestionable.

Isn't it exciting to realize that God has this gift all ready for any one of us who will meditate on His Word! We, too, can have more understanding than our teachers. (What a verse for homework-harried students to latch on to!)

James, likewise, had this concept. "If any of you lack wisdom, let him ask of God," he advises (James 1:5a).

Sometimes we look to the wrong source for what we need, falsely expecting the world to reveal what only the Spirit of God can show us. For instance, for sheer, unadulterated wisdom what college course can begin to measure up to what reading *and meditating* on the book of Proverbs has to offer?

It takes time. It calls for diligence and persistence. But no matter how simple we think we are, we can be wise—with God-given wisdom.

WHO NEEDS A HOROSCOPE?

BIBLE READING: Psalm 1

The Lord knoweth the way of the righteous (v. 6a).

Increasingly, even Christians are becoming intrigued by the horoscope columns in the daily newspapers.

"I was horrified," a young mother admitted, "when I realized that I could hardly wait to get my hands on the paper and turn to the horoscopes each morning. I let it set the tone for my whole day, good or bad. It was like some form of addiction, and I couldn't break away from it until

I confessed it to the Lord and asked Him for help to turn from this habit. Actually," she said, "until this thing got such hold on me, I had unfailingly spent some time each morning reading my Bible and having a quiet time with the Lord. Oh, I'm so glad God wouldn't let me get hooked any further."

This honest young Christian woman hit the nail on the head. People do become addicted to this thing of trying to find what their future holds, whether through the "stars" in their daily paper or by other means. (I must interject here that in a single day, riding a commuter train and picking up three newspapers left by departing passengers, I read three separate, completely contradictory horoscopes for the same "signs." Perhaps it would be good if some gullible people, who are so sold on them, would see the same contradictions.)

As believers in God as our daily Guide, who needs a horoscope reading? Who needs to walk in the counsel of the ungodly? Has not God promised, *I will instruct thee and teach thee in the way which thou shalt go: I will guide thee with mine eye?* (Psalm 32:8).

In a sense, a Christian slaps God in the face by choosing to seek so-called guidance from the horoscope peddlers. Our tomorrows are in the Lord's hands. He knows the way we will take.

Who needs a horoscope?

GOD WILL LET YOU BE INDEPENDENT

BIBLE READING: Philippians 4:13-19

My God shall supply all your need (v. 19).

The pastor's wife turned from the mailbox at the end of the parsonage driveway. She sighed, and her feet dragged.

"Three days in a row and nothing but a mid-winter sale catalog," she said ruefully.

The little mission church congregation was not able to support a pastor; yet it was a needy area that deserved a full-time minister. And, up to this point, he and his wife had not suffered. As they had relied on the Lord and served Him, He had met their daily needs.

Gradually, however, Pastor and Mrs. Smith began to look to the *sources* God used, rather than to God Himself. If a certain person sent them a check to meet the heating costs in January, their prayer was, in effect, "Lord, remind this person that February is a cold month, too."

They were pretty much scraping the bottom of the barrel. The people who had hitherto been faithful in supporting them seemed to have forgotten them. Things were beginning to be desperate, and so were their prayers, when one day a letter arrived with some money in it, not a check that identified the sender. It was cash, and the postmark was quite unfamiliar to either of them. Just one sentence was written on the sheet of paper that enclosed the bills: "Your heavenly Father knows what things you have need of" (Matthew 6:8).

The husband and wife looked at each other. They needed no words to express what they later confessed, that their trust had been in everyone *but* their heavenly Father.

God will let us go it alone if that's how we want it. But the going may get rough. The sources we rely on may all dry up. Not so "God's riches in glory by Christ Jesus." It pays to depend on *God's* supply.

THE KING IS COMING

BIBLE READING: 1 Thessalonians 4:14-18

I will come again (John 14:3).

There's a fresh breeze of prophetic truth blowing these days. Bumper stickers proclaim the good news on our streets and highways: "The King Is Coming." Christian radio broadcasts the beautiful song, "The King Is Coming." Books on prophecy are breaking bestseller records.

Not only are Evangelicals speaking and writing about it, but even the secular world can be heard speculating about some possibly imminent great event, which could be the coming of Jesus Christ as prophesied.

And people are willing, and some are eager, to hear about Christ's second coming.

Is it that the world is weary of *bad* news? Perhaps this blessed hope provides the only possible light at the end of the tunnel?

My own experience is a prime example of how the fascination of this truth can grip a person when he hears it for the first time. It was with an almost total lack of Bible background I heard of Christ's coming back to earth. I found it much more exciting and intriguing than science fiction! It was the hook the Holy Spirit used to get me to listen, to believe, and to be ready for that great day that is coming.

This news that the King is coming is a tremendous evangelistic approach. Secondly, it is a great factor for keeping us close to the Lord. "Every man that has this hope *purifies* himself" (1 John 3:3). To quote Dr. Vernon McGee on his "Through the Bible" radio broadcast, "If this teaching of the second coming of Christ doesn't change you, you'd better go study something else."

"*I will come again*," Jesus said unequivocally; and to me there is no more thrilling, more hope-filled hymn of the church than "Christ Returneth" by H. L. Turner: "It may be at morn, when the day is awaking—"

One of these days, we may be singing and *experiencing*, "Christ returneth! Hallelujah! Hallelujah! Amen."

WAIT A LITTLE WHILE

BIBLE READING: Psalm 130

I wait for the Lord, . . . and in his word do I hope (v. 5).

How often do we hear, "God always answers our prayer; His answer may be yes, or it may be no, or it may be Wait a little while."

From childhood we generally bristle at this "wait a while," and the years do not always bring a measure of maturity that makes waiting acceptable to us. We don't like to play the waiting game.

David, the psalmist, can teach us a thing or two about waiting. In this lovely psalm he paints a picture with which we can all identify: waiting "more than they that watch for the morning." Oh, the long night when we are watching for the morning! It may be a night of anxious watching over a sick loved one or waiting with the dying. At other times it seems that morning will never come because of the long-anticipated joy the morning will bring.

Another kind of waiting is when we're in need of guidance, and it seems the Lord is long in sending us His assurance, "This is the way." This waiting is never easy, and some grow impatient and fail this test. They go ahead on their own, tired of waiting. Maybe later, they will realize and lament, "If I had only waited!"

Sometimes a waiting time is necessary to bring to light certain facts for our good.

Perhaps the greatest test while we wait is that of uncertainty. "I don't mind the waiting if I only could know the outcome," is our very human reaction. Again, David has a word for us in this psalm. "I wait for the Lord, my soul doth wait, and in his word do I hope." David had learned how to possess his soul in patience. It's not how long we wait, but our attitude as we wait, that has its effect upon our tolerance and thus upon our well-being.

Isn't patiently waiting on God a mark of our trust in Him?

THE CHRISTIAN'S MEMORY BANK

BIBLE READING: John 14:18-27

The Holy Spirit . . . will, . . . remind you of everything I . . . have told you (v. 26b, TLB).

How often in a time of deep stress or specific need, a Bible verse plucked from our memory bank has made the difference between hope and despair!

If we would ever be tempted to doubt the transcendent worth of "hiding God's Word in our heart [and mind]," all we need do is listen to a returned Christian POW who spent years in an enemy camp. Without exception these men agree that it was verses and portions from the Bible that helped them maintain not only their spiritual life and integrity but also their mental balance. Some of their greatest feats of ingenuity were in finding ways to communicate to others in solitary confinement another Bible verse one of their number had remembered. They would endanger their lives and suffer torture for the great satisfaction of sharing what the Holy Spirit brought to their remembrance.

21

It's important to keep in mind that we can only cull from our memory that which has been programmed into it. The Holy Spirit does not recall for us something we never knew. So while the opportunity is ours, while we have a good mind and the freedom to read and absorb God's Word, what better security can we be providing for our future than to soak up the Scriptures?

The POWs were impressed that not only the parts they had memorized deliberately but also the things they had been taught in Sunday school and had (in some instances) long forgotten came to their minds to hearten them. This was also true of many hymns.

You may think yourself "not too good at memory work." This is where the Holy Spirit's ministry comes in. God knows our abilities; He has given them to us. And if memorizing is difficult for you, just read and ask God to program His Word into your mind as you read it. It will be there in the bank—against the day of special need, perhaps against the day of famine of the Word of God.

THE RIGHT START IN LIFE

BIBLE READING: Ephesians 6:10-18

Take, . . . the sword of the Spirit, which is the word of God (v. 17).

We're a "right start" people. The right baby food, the right pediatrician, the right first-grade teacher, the right first impressions, et cetera. All this because we recognize the long-range value of right beginnings.

Yet, we are less consistent in the realm of the spiritual. We sometimes fail to give the new convert the right start. For example, a young woman came to see her pastor's wife. "I'm giving up," she said. "I can't live up to the standard of a Christian. I quit!" A wistful look came over her face. "No, I guess I flunked out."

A little gentle questioning of and listening to the troubled person brought her problem to light. Somehow, whether from the pulpit or by her own misunderstanding of what she thought Christianity really is, this new convert had gotten a bad start in her Christian life. She had the false impression that, having accepted Jesus as her Saviour, she would have no more problems nor would she ever be tempted again. So, when a problem arose and—worse— when she succumbed to temptation, immediately she felt she had failed the Lord and that surely she was so unworthy that He would not love her anymore.

She had not been taught that the Christian life is a warfare, that we have a known, recognizable enemy, and that we need to be forearmed. Nor did she know that temptation will come but that God has provided a means of escape (1 Corinthians 10:13).

Many new converts come (as I did) from non-Christian homes. As more mature believers we can help them to have a good start and perhaps prevent some from becoming spiritual drop-outs. By making the Bible truths relevant in their lives, we will also reinforce our own spiritual bulwarks.

THE WORTH OF A DAY PLAN

BIBLE READING: Psalm 103:1-5

And as thy days, so shall thy strength be (Deuteronomy 33:25*b*).

"A woman's work is never done!" How often we either think it or say it. Ask any homemaker what one of the greatest sources of frustration to her is, and she is likely to reply, "I never quite get done all I plan to do any day."

The same can, no doubt, be said of the business person, the student, the teacher, the pastor or missionary, the writer—practically everybody.

Can it be that we have unrealistic day plans?

As we read the account of Creation, one thing stands out: God had a day plan from the first day on through the sixth day, each with specific acts of creation. And God saw His work as good. One day's work for one day: no more, no less.

And the Lord is obviously interested in our activities by the day. According to the Scriptures, He parcels out the strength we need by the day. Have you thought that this does not only mean physical strength but mental and emotional strength as well? Frequently, we can summon the physical effort, but our mind is weary, or we are emotionally under stress. A lack of strength would indicate we have used up our quota for the day, don't you think?

Organization always defeats the lack of organization, and God, who is not the author of confusion but of peace and order, would teach us to plan by the day, to count on His strength by the day, and by His grace to see our work as *good* at the end of each day.

And tomorrow we can tap God's reservoir of strength, for tomorrow will then be "today."

GOD'S SANDPAPER

BIBLE READING: Hebrews 12:9-12

Nevertheless afterward (v. 11).

Any amateur painter knows how irksome is the job of sandpapering—rub-rub-rub. It would be so much simpler, we think, just to slap on a new coat of paint. Nevertheless, we would agree that the sandpapering has a fine effect and that the end result certainly justifies all the effort.

It's like that with us, too, as Christians.

We tend to resist the abrasive circumstances it takes to make some of us smoother, more attractive, easier to live with. Unquestionably, we would opt for gentler means, but they might not be effective in changing us.

The apostle Paul had a realistic attitude toward God's "sandpapering." He viewed such experiences as "working for him": "Our light affliction, which is but for a moment, worketh for us a far more exceeding and eternal weight of glory" (2 Corinthians 4:17).

God is honored in our lives when we, too, take the long view of the irksome or painful processes by which we become what God wants us to be. The Lord is no capricious artist or designer who might possibly change His mind about us and abandon us still unfinished. (Anyone who has been exposed to the concepts of the Bill Gothard Seminars in Basic Youth Conflicts has had this vital encouragement programmed into him: "God is not finished with you yet.")

God knows what He is doing with us and for us: *For I know the thoughts that I think toward you, saith the Lord, thoughts of peace, and not of evil, to give you an expected end* (Jeremiah 29:11).

In the light of our prospects, we can put up with God's sandpapering, can't we?

THE CURE FOR FRETTING

BIBLE READING: Psalm 37:1-8

Rest in the Lord (v. 7).

One of the most beautiful arias of the church is "O Rest in the Lord" from "The Elijah" by Felix Mendelssohn. Like the psalm from which its words derive, it's not only beautiful but also practical.

The Lord really must not want us to fret, for three times

in these eight verses, we read, "Fret not thyself." *Fret* is one word that paints gloomy pictures; it's such a negative-sounding word.

We all fret at some time, of course, but the chronic fretter is one of the most difficult persons to help; his problems seem so vague and undefined. And it's futile just to say to such a person, "Don't fret," or, "Stop fretting." He would if he could. But when God says, "Fret not," that's different, for He gives us both the preventive measures and the cure.

Here is God's prescription for the fretful:

1. *Trust in the Lord.* Check the source of your fear. Is the fear of want causing you to fret?

2. *Delight yourself in the Lord.* Think of the far-reaching promise given when you delight yourself in Him.

3. *Commit your way unto the Lord.* Make the safest of all safety deposits. It savors of Paul's assurance, "I know whom I have believed, and am persuaded that he is able to keep that which I have committed" (2 Timothy 1:12).

4. *Rest in the Lord and wait patiently for him.* Practice patience to defeat a spirit of fretfulness and produce inner rest. The only true rest comes from the Lord. "I will give you rest," Jesus said (Matthew 11:28-29).

5. *Cease from anger.* Examine yourself to see if a lot of your fretfulness is an expression of anger. The Lord bids us to forsake it, give it up voluntarily, and fret not.

With such a trustworthy prescription, have we any real excuse for fretting?

SOMETHING TO BELIEVE IN

BIBLE READING: John 14:1-6

The truth shall make you free (John 8:32).

"All I wanted was to be free. I was *searching for freedom*," explained the young man arraigned before a judge.

At the same time one of the youth's contemporaries was pleading, "I was just trying to find *something I could believe in.*"

If they had only known!

It's so sad that people, old as well as young, earnestly pursue freedom. Jesus said, "You shall know the truth, and the truth shall make you free." It sounds simple. But multitudes today are asking, "Where in all of this planet can we find truth?" Truth becomes a more scarce commodity every day, or so it seems to most people; credibility gaps widen daily in so many areas of life.

Do we give up then and decide that truth is a will o' the wisp, a mirage to disillusion us?

Oh no! No person need go through life fruitlessly searching for truth in order to find freedom. The same Jesus who said, "The truth shall make you free," also stated, "*I am the truth.*" And there is a simple law of mathematics that says, "Things equal to the same thing are equal to each other."

We can conclude, then, that since freedom is found in truth, and Jesus Himself is Truth; then freedom is found in Jesus.

However, our Lord Jesus Christ is no cold, impersonal mathematical equation. He is living, loving, compassionate, approachable. He is the Truth that we can know in our *hearts*, not only in our heads.

It's not enough for us to know mentally that Jesus *is* the Truth and thus the source of the only true freedom humanity can ever know. We must know Him as the Way, the Truth, and the Life; know Him as our personal Saviour, our Emancipator from sin. This is true freedom—and something (Someone) to believe in.

NO AMATEURS PERMITTED

BIBLE READING: Ephesians 2:18-22

I will build my church (Matthew 16:18).

Heavenly analogies are all around us if we are alert to recognize them.

Not long ago, a friend and I were making our daily "sidewalk inspection" of a new building at the Narramore Christian Foundation. The contractor, a friend of ours, was off the job at the time. We watched as a bricklayer labored so carefully and with such precision: then my friend asked if she might lay a brick. "Just one—so I can say I had a part in the new building," she begged. The answer was no, but the workman graciously explained how important it was that each brick be laid exactly right, that much depended on this.

The following day, having heard about us and the bricks, the contractor met us and said, "How would you like to hammer a nail in this woodwork? Then you can say you had a part in the building." So we each pounded our nail and went on our way, satisfied.

It was later that day that the beautiful analogy dawned on me. Even though the contractor was our friend, we could not be permitted to hazard the perfection of the finished building. Only a master builder could be trusted to lay the bricks. I thought of Christ's words, "I will build my church." Not Peter. Not Paul. Not any of the great Bible preachers of the past. Not Dwight L. Moody or Billy Graham. Christ alone fitly frames together, not bricks, but *living stones* (1 Peter 2:5) for His spiritual house. Who but Christ knows where each one belongs? Who but Christ knows those who are truly His and are acceptable "building materials"?

To my mind also came the heart-warming truth that the Lord lets us "hammer a nail", have some little part in the building of His church. He graciously allows us to gather material for His church as we faithfully witness and "bring them in." But the building itself is the responsibility of God's Master Builder. And the gates of hell shall not prevail against it.

WHAT ARE YOU WEARING?

BIBLE READING: 1 Peter 3:1-6

The ornament of a meek and quiet spirit (v. 4).

Sometimes a hymn stamps an indelible image on our minds. I think of one I heard for the first time at a monthly class meeting of an adult Bible class. I cannot recall having heard it more than a couple of times since.

The class teacher read the first verse that began:

> I want the adorning divine;
> I want in His likeness to shine.

We sang right through this hymn, and lines from the last verse captivated me as had those in the first:

> I want—and this sums up my prayer,
> To glorify Thee till I die.*

There was no mistaking the sincerity of this teacher. Within a week, without prior illness, she passed on into the presence of her Lord. Hers was an impressive funeral. The guard of honor was made up of boys and girls from her city-wide Bible clubs. The most prominent floral piece bore a tribute: "To our dear teacher who loved us and taught us to love Jesus."

She had glorified Him till she died. She now wears "the adorning divine."

*From *Sankey's Sacred Songs and Solos,* used by permission of Marshall, Morgan & Scott Publications.

29

We don't use the word "adorning" anymore (if we ever did). But we can't escape its connotation for us in Paul's use of the word. Everyone of us "wears" what other people both see and sense. They make their judgment of us accordingly, not only of us as individuals—whether family members or neighbors or friends—but also of what we believe and of what is important to us.

And for maximum effectiveness in witnessing, "a gentle and quiet spirit" (Berkeley) has top priority.

As believers our ultimate adorning divine is assured.

And *today* we can glorify God.

THE VALUE OF BEING FLEXIBLE

BIBLE READING: Acts 16:7-13

Immediately we endeavored to go (v. 10).

Your plans are all made. You have prayed, and you feel at peace sensing the leading of the Lord.

Then—something happens. An emergency arises that involves you directly. What should you do? What *do* you do?

At this point you have a choice. You can dig in your heels and affirm to everybody that you have your own plans all laid, that you can't possibly change your schedule, no matter what.

Or you can pause and take stock. Ask, "Lord, are You speaking to me in this situation? What do You want me to do? I can afford to be flexible just as long as I know that You are leading me."

Circumstances differ. There are times when we have to be firm and unmoveable. The Holy Spirit gives us the discernment to recognize that what has happened is not, in fact, a crisis involving us, but rather a detour to steer us away from God's purpose for us.

The clue in the situation is to be willing to be led by the Holy Spirit. He will never lead us contrary to God's will for us, nor will He lead us to do less than God's will.

Paul, unquestionably, must have felt he was in the will of God when he headed for Bithynia. We are not told how "the Spirit suffered him not", how God changed Paul's direction geographically. But He did! Suppose at that point Paul had argued, been adamant, declaring, "I'm going to *Bithynia;* I will not be turned aside or be dissuaded."

History never reveals its alternatives; so, we can only speculate as to what would have happened to world history if Paul had disregarded the call to Macedonia and failed to take the gospel into Europe at that time. But Paul was flexible. He could afford to scrap his own plans and make new travel arrangements, since God was in command of the situation.

There's a time for everything, said Solomon.

So there's a time for you to be flexible in order that God's perfect will be done in your life.

FORTUNE COOKIE FAITH

BIBLE READING: Joshua 1:6-8; Psalm 1:2

In his law doth he meditate (Psalm 1:2*b*).

Have you met people who tend to open the Bible at random, glance over the page to which they turn, and expect to receive direction and guidance from God? Usually such people complain, "I don't seem to get anything out of the Bible."

A friend of mine has an answer for them. "You're looking for a fortune cookie," he tells them, "and God is not in the fortune cookie business."

To a degree, I suspect that we are all guilty of this practice of playing "Bible eeny-meeny," even though we have the exhortation to study the Word of God and to meditate on it. Verse-grabbing, in an attempt to meet our spiritual need or to find help in a time of crisis, is a poor substitute for knowing the Scriptures so well that we can turn to a particular portion for comfort and guidance.

Nevertheless, God is God, and in His grace and mercy He meets us at our point of need. There are too many specific instances of people having been helped as they opened to a page of the Bible and a verse leapt out at them for us to doubt that this does happen. No doubt you can cite some such experience yourself, as I can. After all, we have the words of Jesus that our Father will not give us a stone when we ask for bread.

But no one would expect to subsist on fortune cookies. Neither can we, as believers, have God's best in our lives if we will not discipline ourselves to study to show ourselves approved unto Him (2 Timothy 2:15). We need the milk and the meat of the Word daily. We need to chew it and digest it in order to build spiritual muscles as it becomes a part of us.

Dr. Clyde Narramore tells that as a young man, growing up on a ranch, he would go to a sorghum patch and cut some "chewing pieces," before he started a day's work. The little sticks of sweetness provided enjoyment throughout the day. In like manner, we can meditate on the Word of God that we have hidden in our hearts, and it becomes like honey for sweetness.

Who wants to settle for an unpredictable fortune cookie?

COME TO THE FOUNTAIN

BIBLE READING: Isaiah 44:1-4; 55:1

I will pour water on him that is thirsty (v. 3).

Driving through the southwestern United States with its ever-changing landscape, the traveler cannot fail to be impressed with the vital difference that water-irrigation makes. The right side of the highway may be lush and green; the left side is, to quote a Parks Department official, "only fit for sage brush and jack rabbits."

Prolonged drought creates this desert.

There is, likewise, a drought that creates a desert of the soul and spirit. But this need not be—not with such promises as the Lord made through Isaiah!

"Ho, everyone that thirsteth, come ye to the waters" (Isaiah 55:1).

And what of Christ's inviting offer, "If any man thirst, let him come unto me" (John 7:37)?

Thirst is a demon sensation. People will do almost anything to slake their thirst.

As Christians we need not be "thirsty," drought-ridden, unproductive, and spiritually useless to God—and to our neighbor who may need some spillover from us.

Addressing a group of Christian writers at the Mount Hermon Writers' Conference, Dr. Sherwood Wirt, editor of *Decision* magazine, counseled his hearers to "let the Word of God irrigate your mind every day." Surely here is a preventative for dryness and fruitless work!

It's easy for people to detect when we have been to the fountain, been refreshed in soul, in mind, in spirit. We have an aliveness, a buoyancy that's sadly missing when we neglect to partake of the water of the Word.

The lovely hymn, "Ho, Everyone That Is Thirsty," bids us,

Come to the fountain, there's fullness in Jesus;
While you are seeking Him, He will be found.

LUCY RYDER MEYER*

*From *Sankey's Sacred Songs and Solos,* used by permission.

THE TRIPLE QUESTION

BIBLE READING: John 21:15-19

Do you love me? (v. 15, TLB).

Among the current rash of "love" bumper stickers, posters, and greeting cards, this questioning couplet caught my eye:

> Do you love me, or do you not?
> You told me once—but I forgot.

There's a pathos about this "You told me once."

How convincing can a one-time telling of something important be, especially in these days of repetitive bombardment?

We hear much from child psychologists concerning the vital, lifetime import of telling your child you love him, of telling again and again.

But we hear few if any voices urging us to tell the Lord Jesus Christ we love Him. Of course, He knows our hearts. He knows if or when we "once told Him we love Him." He has not forgotten.

Suppose, though, that God had told us just once, "I love you." And forever after, we had to go on this one-time assurance, while all kinds of other voices beat in on us in an effort to cause us to forget or to doubt God's love for us.

God was careful to see that this did not happen. He spelled out His love for us through Christ's death on the cross. And He recorded in writing the fact of His love that we might be continually reinforced in our assurance.

> I find myself pondering,
> How else had we heard
> Had not God in His Word
> Said "I LOVE YOU"?*

*Jeanette Lockerbie, *Tomorrow's at My Door* (Old Tappan, N.J.: Revell, 1973), p. 28. Used by permission.

Can we not, then, in turn say to our Lord, "I love—love You—*love* You"?

BAROMETER RISING

BIBLE READING: Psalm 42:5-11

Why art thou cast down (v. 5).

Aren't you glad life offers opportunities for change?

Suppose, for instance, that once the barometer starts to fall, there's no way it could ever swing upward again. What a gloomy prospect!

What if, when our spirits droop (as droop they will), there were no possibility that they could ever soar up from the depths? If we are honest with ourselves, we will admit that, emotionally, we sometimes register "cloudy" or "stormy," for life does bring clouds of grief and storms of threatening fears.

David, the Psalmist, experienced such times when his personal barometer read "low and falling." He frequently recognized that he was downcast in spirit. This thread runs through a number of the recorded episodes of his life.

Fortunately, David also recognized that there is a way up. He did not continue to wallow in his personal slough of despondency. Nor need you or I. For, when we let depression engulf us, we affect not only ourselves but also those around us, much in the manner of a sunless day. And we're certainly not much of a testimony for God at that point.

So, let's consider David's formula for dispelling gloom. *"Hope thou in God,"* he counseled his own spirit—and ours.

Hope is an uplifting word. Just to say it acts as a tonic for our spirits.

Dark and difficult days will come. Well did Annie Johnson Flint write, "God hath not promised skies always blue."

But we know that God has promised to be with us in trouble (Psalm 91:15) and what God promises He delivers. (Note that God did not promise to keep us from trouble, but to keep us in the midst of it.)

Isn't that sufficient impetus to our falling or failing spirits? Doesn't such assurance change the direction of our emotional and spiritual barometers?

PUBLIC ACKNOWLEDGEMENT

BIBLE READING: Matthew 10:24-33

If anyone publicly acknowledges me as his friend, I will openly acknowledge him as my friend before my father in heaven (v. 32, TLB).

Becky is a new Christian. Visiting with her neighbors over coffee, she very openly shared with them the wonderful change that knowing Jesus had made in her life. Her sparkling eyes and bubbling enthusiasm spoke well for her newfound faith.

Later, chatting with another Christian, Becky mentioned this experience. To her complete amazement, the woman's response was anything but joyful.

"How did they take it?" she asked (*as though it were medicine*, Becky thought). Without waiting for a reply to her question the other person, an older Christian, added, "What will they think of you?"

Becky blinked a time or two. She could scarcely believe this negative attitude. All she could think to reply was, "I never thought anything about what they would think of me, *really*. After all, I would be happy to recommend my doctor, or my dentist, or pediatrician. And if I know about where to find something somebody's looking for in a store, I'm always quick to tell them. So, why wouldn't I want to tell my neighbors about my best Friend!"

Sometimes it takes babes in Christ to convey such a message to those of us who are older in the faith and perhaps more staid. And to our shame we may have to confess to the Lord that we have not been recommending Him, have not been publicly acknowledging Him before our friends and neighbors.

Why do some of us find this so difficult to do? Like Becky, we're no doubt willing enough to help other people by recommending various products and people and services. Can it be that this other Christian zeroed in on our real problem in witnessing: "What will 'they' think of us?" "Will we appear different from our neighbors who are not believers and thus be persona non grata?" To that the Scripture replies, "The disciple is not above his master."

And think of the position that will be ours when, one day, Jesus calls us "friend" before His Father in heaven. Public acknowledgement indeed—and just for recommending the Friend of sinners!

MAKING THE RIGHT IMPRESSION

BIBLE READING: 2 Corinthians 6:1-6

By kindness, . . . by love unfeigned (v. 6).

Jeannie and her suburbanite neighbors were discussing what they had been trained for and what they were doing with their skills and abilities. They represented an impressive array of diversified training.

"What about you, Jeannie?" one of the young women asked. "You haven't told us where your talents lie."

"I don't think you would be too impressed," Jeannie, the only Christian in the group, answered.

"Oh, c'mon," one of the others said. "You have lots of talents."

"Name two," Jeannie challenged them, with a grin.

"You can write; I know that," one neighbor spoke up. "That's *one*."

"She said 'two,'" another girl quipped.

The next few minutes were a revelation to this young Christian woman.

"Jeannie has the unusual ability to make other people feel good—me, for instance."

"I can always come to you when something's bothering me, Jeannie," said one of the others, "and you *listen*. That's a talent you have."

"You're kind and thoughtful of other people."

Only God knew how often Jeannie had prayed for these neighbors of hers, had prayed that the Lord would help her be the kind of person in her contacts with them that would be a right image of Christianity.

And now this! "Thank You, Lord," she was silently praying, her heart singing. "Thank You for making the right impression through Your Holy Spirit in me."

Not always do we, as Christians, have the joyful gratification of knowing how we are being used for good in other people's lives. But sometimes we do. In this instance the message comes through loud and clear. Talents? Abilities? What are people really looking for? Kindness. Warmth. Loving understanding. And by His Spirit, the Lord will help each of us make the right impression.

ONE WAY

BIBLE READING: John 14:1-6

I am the way (v. 6).

We Christians in the seventies have our distinct symbol: the upraised finger indicating "One Way"—a simple gesture of fellowship between believers.

But what about our unsaved neighbors who may observe this little byplay, knowing nothing of what it means. What does "One Way" say to the uninitiated?

Our Lord made the way to heaven so plain He could have said, "You can't miss it." But a whole world of people around us are missing the way.

"But I've tried to share Christ with my neighbor," you may be saying, "and she comes back with her argument that her way is just as good as mine."

We can expect to meet with such resistance, but that doesn't change the facts, nor does it absolve us of the responsibility to keep on witnessing.

Sometimes we tend to fudge around rather than being explicit. An example might be when someone asks, "What does 'One Way' mean?" and we look a bit uncomfortable, explain that it has to do with our church—and let it go at that. Suppose we were to say to someone who asks directions to a particular place, "You just go a few blocks then turn either right or left at the first convenient intersection, then drive a mile or two. You can't miss it"!

Ridiculous? Yes, and worse, such distorted directions would throw the person into confusion, cost her valuable time, and possibly result in her never reaching her desired destination. No one can afford to miss the way to Jesus Christ and to heaven. So, we may find that we have to repeat the directions again and again (especially for people like me who have a hard time understanding directions).

God has made the way clear. So clear and plain that, as Isaiah the prophet puts it (speaking of the highway of holiness), "that wayfaring men, though fools, need not err therein" (Isaiah 35:8).

As God's representatives we, too, need to keep the directions simple, so simple that even our most uninformed neighbor can grasp this vital truth: that Jesus is Himself the Way—*the* Way. One Way.

THANKS, GOD, I NEEDED THAT

BIBLE READING: Psalm 34:1-3

In everything give thanks (1 Thessalonians 5:18).

Has it ever occurred to you that we can cure a significant number of our ills—especially emotional ills—by the therapy of a thankful spirit?

We can.

By "a thankful spirit" I'm not referring in any way to a Pollyanna attitude. I mean a genuinely thankful spirit, the "being thankful for everything" because we accept it as a part of God's plan for our lives.

God never issues a directive in His Word that He does not mean us to take seriously and carry out. Neither does He ask us to do anything He will not enable us to do. By His grace in our lives we can say with David: "I will bless the Lord *at all times.*" With Job we repeat, "The Lord gave, and the Lord hath taken away; blessed be the name of the Lord" (Job 1:21).

The Christian who continuously has such a spirit of thankfulness toward God is, in effect, saying:

"Lord, I know I belong to You and that You love me and have a plan for my life. So I'm accepting this trial as from Yourself. It's not something I would choose, and I can't see or understand the reason for it. I can't even figure how any good can come out of it. But You know. So, thank You, Lord."

Faith fed on the promises of God and coupled to our past experiences with Him latches on to the hope, "Not now, but afterwards." And this *faith* and this *hope*—because they are anchored in Christ—produce a great *peace.*

This is the peace that passes understanding, Christ's special legacy to the believer (John 14:27). It passes the understanding of our neighbors who shake their heads and say, "I don't know how you can bear—whatever the trial."

Then, by our thankful spirit, our acceptance of what God sends our way, we can be the best possible witnesses to the fact that Christianity is viable, that it works for us.

And, in God's own time, we generally can look back and say, "Thanks for that particular experience, Lord. I needed it."

IT IS ENOUGH TO MAKE THE BELLS RING

BIBLE READING: Luke 15:1-10

That likewise joy shall be in heaven (v. 7).

Have you ever lost something you really prized? Then when you had despaired of ever finding it again, there it was!

I recall the time I lost the diamond out of my engagement ring. Like the woman in Luke 15 I diligently sought for it, turned on the light, and swept the house. But it seemed so futile. I had almost resigned myself that I would never see that diamond again when, shining a flashlight into a dark spot between the kitchen cupboards, I saw the little stone winking at me. And I'll always remember my joy in finding it.

But that's a poor illustration of what Jesus was teaching that day when He spoke of a lost sheep and a lost piece of silver. These were merely preamble to the real lesson: the worth of a soul in the sight of God.

Sometimes one of the beautiful thoughts in this "parable of lost things" is not emphasized. It's this: in the story of the shepherd just one was lost. This shepherd still had his ninety and nine sheep. And as the hymn "The Ninety and Nine" by Elizabeth Clephane so beautifully phrases it, "Are they not enough for Thee?" No! The ninety-nine were not enough. One was lost, and the search had to be continued until the number was complete; the one hundred sheep, not ninety-nine, could satisfy the shepherd.

And so one piece of silver was missing? The woman had nine pieces left. Why fuss and bother to find just one piece?

The story goes on. A certain man had two sons. To be sure, one left home, but his elder son stayed with him on the farm. However, for this father, who is emblematic of the heavenly Father, as long as one son was missing, there was no joy in the home. However, the father kept on loving his wayward son; and we can imagine that day after day he strained his eyes watching the horizon to see if his younger son was coming home. That day eventually came, and it was enough to make bells ring.

> Ring the bells of heaven; there is joy today
> For a soul returning from the wild.
>
> W. O. CUSHING

There is joy in heaven over *one* sinner that repenteth. By our witness to our unsaved neighbors, we can have a part in making heaven's bells ring.

GREAT EXPECTATIONS

BIBLE READING: Psalm 37:1-5

No good thing will He withhold from them that walk uprightly (Psalm 84:11).

Edith, a smiling, happy Christian, can be counted on to greet her friends with this question, "Had any spiritual surprises lately?" Sometimes she calls these surprises "serendipities," and her tone when she asks always indicates that she expects a yes answer.

This is a good question worth pondering. It's my personal belief that God delights in giving surprises to His children, as much as or more than an earthly father does.

Even the concept has great value in our life; with its Christmas morning feeling it creates a sense of something good about to happen. This prevents us from always looking on the gloomy side.

You and I know people who go through life expecting only the worst. Let a telegram be delivered, and these people immediately are mentally donning black, even before opening the envelope. They're perpetually tuned to the trouble channel. When these are professing Christians, what a let-down they must be to their unsaved neighbors who have only them for models of what a Christian is.

By contrast, my "spiritual surprises" friend and others whom she has influenced are a savor of good things; they project a true image of our loving Father in heaven.

We are exhorted to delight ourselves in the Lord; and in turn, we can believe that God will delight Himself in us, and no good thing will He withhold from us (Psalm 84: 11). I believe it pleases God to have us wake up in the morning with the feeling, "I know You're going to bless me today, Lord; and I can hardly wait for Your spiritual surprises."

Our great expectations can color our entire day; color it bright. And we can never expect more than God is waiting to give us. Why then don't we make great expectations a way of life?

MILLION DOLLAR FAITH

BIBLE READING: 2 Corinthians 9:6-11

My God shall supply (Philippians 4:19).

The speaker at the Christian Women's Club luncheon was relating an experience of the Lord's miraculous provision when she prayed for five thousand dollars to meet a particular need. Seated in her audience, another Christian woman was pondering, *If I ever ask the Lord for money, I'll ask Him for a million!* And in her mind she began to apportion the money, beginning with buying land for a children's camp. This was a project in which she had long been interested.

Before long, this woman did pray for a million dollars. It's too long a story to go into here, but she is a living testimony today to the fact that God did give her a million dollars. And in numerous ways that I know of, and undoubtedly many more that only God knows about, she is proving herself a good steward of this vast sum with which God has entrusted her.

James wrote, "Ye have not because ye ask not" (James 4:2).

Not many of us are going to ask the Lord for one million dollars. But perhaps we can increase our requests a little bit, in keeping with the God who is able. We are quick to quote Philippians 4:19. And, if you are like me, you see the first part in capital letters, MY GOD SHALL SUPPLY ALL YOUR NEEDS—and the rest of it just rolls off your tongue because it's part of a verse you have memorized. But think of it! God's provision is *according to His riches.* Why should we limit Him? Why not ask for large petitions? Would giving a million dollars impoverish the God of the universe?

I believe it delights Almighty God to have us, His people, stretch our faith toward His ability to provide, not toward human resources.

It may be that it's not material needs that keep you on your knees before God. Rather, you may be praying for the salvation of someone dearer than life itself. And it's been a long time. And you are despairing that it will ever happen. I would urge you to pray a "million dollar prayer"; let God know you trust Him for this otherwise impossible answer. And watch God work!

MAKING OUR OPPORTUNITIES

BIBLE READING: 2 Timothy 4:1-7

Instant in season, out of season (v. 2).

Jane turned from her front door where she had politely refused literature from a woman propagating her cult. Then from her window Jane watched the woman determinedly march up to a house across the street and knock on the door.

You have to hand it to her. She's certainly persistent, Jane thought.

Discussing the incident with her family at dinner, she admitted, "I wonder how we would measure up to her in the faithfulness department."

"Oh, Mom!" her teenager parried. "She just goes around knocking on doors because she *has* to. All these cult people have to take a stint at passing out their stuff."

"That shouldn't excuse us for not knocking on doors, son," she answered.

Her husband chipped in, "You take the opportunity to witness for the Lord whenever it comes, Honey. Don't beat yourself over the head."

"That's what bothers me," Jane confessed. "Sure, I take opportunities. But I don't *make* them. You don't find me knocking on a stranger's door in order to share my faith."

Taking the opportunity—or making one.

Perhaps we, too, dismiss the false doctrine peddlers and their persistence, at the same time excusing our own lack of zeal. But what we cannot disregard is that they are "instant in season, and out of season," whatever their motivation. Should we be less diligent? Should we let them outdo us in spreading their "gospel" while we leave our own neighbors untouched by the true Gospel of Jesus Christ?

We can't stop the spread of cultist literature. But we can

take a leaf out of the cultist's book—and start doing some door-knocking ourselves. How about it? Witnessing is always in season.

AROUND THE WORLD—AND AROUND THE CORNER

BIBLE READING: Romans 12:6-13

Who is my neighbor? (Luke 10:29).

Sometimes we reach out around the world in our efforts to win people to Christ (and we *should*), but we need to be mindful of the unsaved right around the corner from us.

To quote Dr. George Sweeting, president of the Moody Bible Institute, "Some people will chase a Greek preposition all over the New Testament, but they won't seek out the lost soul in the next block."

Myra Brown had been in that category, a woman who gloried in her Bible knowledge and spent long hours "chasing Greek prepositions." Then a new house was built just around the corner from hers, and the young newlywed neighbor began to appear at Myra's door almost daily. Sometimes she was in need of directions on how to get somewhere, or she needed an item for a new recipe she was trying. At the time it had never once occurred to Myra that this young woman might be lonely, that she might have just used her "needs" as an excuse for some womanly companionship. All Myra knew was that she was an unwelcome interruption, a bit of a nuisance, in fact.

Until— As she was praying that the Lord would not let the girl come that particular day, Myra had an uneasy feeling come over her. She terminated her prayer and started her regular Bible study. Her project was comparing ver-

sions of Luke. She came that day to chapter 10:29, and in
The Living Bible she read: "The man wanted to justify
(his lack of love for some kinds of people), so he asked,
'Which neighbors?'"

Neighbor. Neighbor. The word kept intruding into
Myra's thoughts. And in her mind's eye, she could see her
young neighbor, Esther, tripping up to her front door, eager,
always with some excuse to come in.

Suddenly, Myra saw herself as she felt God must have
seen her all those times when she was inwardly bristling at
having to give her time, her precious time that she could
be using to study in order to build up her image as a knowl-
edgeable student of the Bible. "Forgive me, Lord," she
prayed, "and thank You for showing me my responsibility
to my neighbor."

That had been some weeks ago. Now, a happy smile
played on Myra's face as she saw Esther hurrying up the
walk. Myra knew who her neighbor was—and now they
were studying the Bible together!

THE COVER UP

BIBLE READING: 1 Peter 3:8-11

Love covereth all sins (Proverbs 10:12).

There's something beautiful about a family who always
speak well of one another, who cover up for each other.
Looking on, people outside such a family envy them for
this deep love and loyalty: not that the members of this
family are blind to each other's faults and sins and shortcomings, but that they keep these strictly in the family.
Their love covers up the failings.

Is this what Peter is appealing for in the family of God?
As brothers and sisters will we so love one another that
we will not stoop to traffic in each other's sins? Love forgives. Love overlooks the other's faults, remembering that

Jesus so loved us that He died to take away our sins. This kind of love is a blanket that completely covers the family sins and shortcomings.

When we don't have this all-enveloping love for one another in Christ, we tend to be critical of others and to cover our own sins. We magnify the negatives and minimize the positive qualities of our fellow Christians. Rather than cover, we expose all of their weaknesses. And when we do, our unsaved neighbors are confused and disappointed. (I sometimes wonder where the non-Christians get all their insight as to what a shining model a Christian should be!) They are longing to be better than they are themselves; and when they see in us things that cause them to question the reality of salvation, they feel let down.

We can afford to cover up for our Christian family members than we can afford not to.

Even if we have not paid attention to this important area of our Christian life, there's hope for us! We have taken the first step when we recognize our failure. Then as we seek God's forgiveness, He will blot out our sins, and He will give us a new love that like a blanket will cover a multitude of [others'] sins (1 Peter 4:8).

SOMEONE'S FOLLOWING YOU

Bible Reading: Philippians 3:13-17

Those things, which ye have, . . . seen in me, do (Philippians 4:9).

Whether we realize it or not, people are watching us and modelling their lives according to what they see in us. Sometimes it is our neighbors.

For a number of years in Brooklyn, New York, I had the most wonderful neighbor. She took an interest in everything our family did in a kindly non-nosy way. One day she said to me, "George and I never go any place anymore without saying a little prayer in the car before we start." I was both delighted and a little surprised, for I did not know her to be a praying woman. She explained, "I've seen you folks get into your car and then sit for a minute with your heads bowed before you set off. Now we do this too, and it makes us feel so safe."

I couldn't help wondering what else this neighbor observed in us as representatives of Christ.

Has the thought ever occurred to you that Paul made a pretty presumptuous proposition when he wrote: "Keep putting into practice all you learned from me and saw me doing" (4:19, TLB).

It would savor of colossal conceit except for the verses in chapter three, especially "No, dear brothers, I am still not all I should be" (3:13, TLB).

Paul could recommend that people follow him because he himself was following his Lord. He could say, "Do what I've taught you; do what you've heard and what you have seen me do."

The crunch comes for most of us when we realize that perhaps what we say—what people *hear* from us—doesn't coincide with what they see us doing.

We need not, however, constantly berate ourselves by saying, "I hope nobody's taking *me* for an example of what a good Christian should be." Rather, so long as, to the best of our knowledge and with the Holy Spirit's guidance, we follow the Lord and keep our eyes on Him, we can confidently let other people follow us, for we will be walking in the footsteps of Jesus.

HOW TO BE A SWEET CHRISTIAN

BIBLE READING: Ezekiel 3:1-4

Take, . . . a little honey (Genesis 43:11).

We hear it said of a person, "She's so sweet." When this sweet person is a Christian, what a fine image of Christ she presents to those around her.

What is "sweet"?

To be considered sweet, do we have to be pretty, talented, popular, accomplished, a certain age, a fashion plate? No! A woman can be any and all of these and still not be sweet. What then is "sweet"? To me, it describes the person with whom I am comfortable, who makes me feel comfortable. She is kind and considerate and thoughtful in a number of ways. And unselfishness is part of being sweet. (It's beginning to line up like "the fruit of the Spirit").

"But I'm not like that. Nobody ever says about me, 'Isn't she sweet?'" Is this what you're saying about yourself as you read this little article? If so, here is the prescription for change: "Take a little honey." I found this verse (Genesis 43:11) almost hidden in the life story of Joseph.

Ezekiel adds his testimony to the formula for becoming sweet. And here is something we can all get in on. As we live close to the Lord, read His Word, and live by it, we find the honey that will make us sweet. Not only will it be pleasant to our own taste, but also it will create in us a new sweetness that we can carry with us wherever we go.

Isn't it significant that the Lord commanded Ezekiel to "eat of the roll" before going out to witness? It was personal preparation for the job God had assigned to him. And the prophet was aware that it made a difference in his life, that it was as honey for sweetness.

We all face people of our own race and nationality, even as Ezekiel was called to minister to his own people. Perhaps we need to replenish our store of honey, be nourished by it ourselves—then carry it with us to our neighbors.

KEEPING THE RECORDING
ANGEL BUSY

Bible Reading: Malachi 3:16-18

A book of remembrance (v. 16).

All we have to do to discover their chief interests in life is to sit and listen to a group of people in a social situation where no particular interest has brought them together.

With predictable regularity, such topics as diets, the high cost of living, television programs, and according to the ages of the persons present, health problems, retirement, or children's problems keep the conversation rolling.

And that is all quite harmless; it's good for people to talk and to have other people to bounce their ideas on. This can prove helpful sometimes.

There's one kind of talking, though, that we can be certain will bring its own reward. But we don't very often take advantage of it. It is as though we compartmentalized our interests: spiritual and secular, "other world" and this world.

We're not guilty of overworking the recording angel.

Yet, we have this tremendous promise in God's Word, one of the very first verses brought to my attention when I came to know Christ as my Saviour: "Then they that feared the Lord spake often" [note that word "often"] one to another: And the Lord . . . heard it, And a book of remembrance was written before him for them. . . . And they shall be mine, saith the Lord of hosts."

When will this be?

> When He cometh, when He cometh
> To make up His jewels.
>
> William O. Cushing

According to the verses in Malachi, this will be a special

recognition for simply thinking upon His name and speaking often one to another about the Lord. And we do not have to wait for the blessing in heaven; there's a special blessing right here and now, as we talk about Him.

THERE IS MY NEIGHBOR!

BIBLE READING: 1 John 3:18-24

If we have love (John 13:35).

In a department store, a young mother suddenly exclaimed to a friend who was shopping with her, "There's my neighbor!"

This would be a common-place incident—except for the light in the woman's face when she made her announcement. I'll let her tell you why this neighbor was so meaningful to her that the very sight of her, even at a distance, brought joy and delight.

"It was the blackest period of my life. My husband had so many problems of his own that he couldn't stand the responsibility of being a husband and father. He walked out on us. I was alone and mixed-up. I had tried a number of religions but got nothing out of them to satisfy either my head or my heart. Across the street lived a family whom I knew to be Christians. And I didn't want to have anything to do with another religion. But they loved us, my children and me, and loved us and loved us. They treated my children as though they were their own and started to take them to church on Sunday. For two years they kept on loving us. Then one Sunday morning I woke up and said to myself, 'What kind of a mother am I? Letting them take my children to their church. Today I'm going myself. I'm going to see what kind of a place it is and what they're teaching my boy and girl.'

"Two years of love—but it took just two weeks of my

going to church. I drank in the message of the love of God for me. I asked God to forgive me and asked Jesus to come into my life and be my Lord and Saviour. This wasn't just some other religion. Oh, no! This was what explained people like my wonderful neighbors. They had the love of Christ in their hearts, and they had literally loved me into joining them."

Perhaps you're thinking, as I did when I heard this story from the young woman herself, *How wonderful it would be to have someone's face light up in such a way at the remembrance of me.* It can happen—if we have love.

YOUR MISSIONARY NEIGHBOR

BIBLE READING: Romans 12:1-5

Be at peace with everyone; just as much as possible (v. 18, TLB).

Nowhere is a good neighbor relationship more important than among missionaries. Yet conditions can, many times, be far from conducive to cordiality. Missionaries are as given to human frailties as the rest of us, and the fact that two neighbors are dedicated Christian workers does not automatically guarantee that they will have an affinity for one another or that they will be compatible.

The problem is generally greater because the missionary is bound into a situation, possibly neighboring in a compound with someone whom she would never have chosen. Negative feelings can surface over their different backgrounds, standards of cleanliness, attitudes toward their own and others' children, Christian taboos, and traits in general.

The missionary is ever conscious of the effect her behavior and attitudes toward her fellow missionaries have on the very people to whom she has come to witness. Consequently, guilt feelings plague her over failure to "love her neighbor" to whom it is so difficult to adjust.

Missionaries need diligent prayer concerning their interpersonal relationships perhaps as much as they do for the seemingly "more spiritual" aspects of their life.

It's not enough to be denominationally "one in the spirit; one in the Lord." It's in the nitty-gritty everyday concerns that the onlooker—the national, Christian or non-Christian—can note the Spirit of Christ at work.

It will take diligent prayer, living by the Word of God, and keeping close to the Lord to maintain the desired unity of the body of Christ.

The Lord never gives a command, however, without supplying the needed grace and strength to obey the command, for those who will appropriate it. "Love your neighbor" has no exclusion clause for missionaries. Our credibility rests on how we treat each other in the family of God, for "By this shall all men know that you are my disciples, if ye have love one to another" (John 13:35).

THE BEST IS YET TO BE

BIBLE READING: 1 Corinthians 2:7-12

Eye hath not seen, nor ear heard (v. 9).

How often we hear people repeat the poet Browning's famous words, "The best is yet to be." We tend to use the phrase most when the person to whom we address it is passing through a time of trial or adversity. And all too often people hear the words through their tears.

Perhaps you've consoled *yourself* at times with "the best is yet to be." And for the Christian there was never a greater word of comfort, never a truer expression of hope and optimism.

But have you thought that these are good words when things are going well for us, when as the saying goes, "We've never had it so good"? Maybe we hadn't. But we will have it better!

No matter how kindly life may treat us, we can look forward to an even better day ahead.

No matter how difficult the journey of life is, the end of the road beckons us on to a beautiful destination, for our Scripture says: "Eye hath not seen, nor ear heard, neither hath it entered into the heart of man, the things which God hath prepared for them that love him."

"But," the apostle goes on to enlighten us, "God hath revealed them to us by His Spirit." So we need not be in the dark as to what is ahead. We can be perfectly assured that the best is yet to be, a "best" that will find us in the place that Jesus has gone to prepare for us. Have you ever wondered what kind of "things" we'll find there? As some Christians have speculated, "When we think what God created in *six days* and then we ponder that nearly two thousand years have passed since Jesus went to prepare a place for us, what kind of place must it be!" Could we ask for more?

Jesus will be there, and we will be with Him. This is "the best that is yet to be."

A LEGACY FOR THE HEART AND MIND

Bible Reading: John 14:25-31

I am leaving you with a gift (v. 27a, TLB).

Suppose you could draw up a will leaving someone dear to you the most important thing in all the world. What would it be?

55

The Bible tells us that Jesus "knew what was in man" (John 3:25), and as Creator, He certainly did. So, when our Lord came to the time of parting from those who were His closest human associates while He walked the shores of time, He left them not just *a* legacy. He left them the one thing which, above everything else, they would need in the days and years ahead. They would need His legacy to them far more than they would need food, clothing, health, preservation from seen and unseen dangers, shelter from the heat and the cold.

"I am leaving you with a gift—peace of mind and heart!" (TLB) Peace—it cannot be bought, nor can we work for it. Here was a gift that would never know devaluation, a gift that was not limited by boundaries of location, of age, or of time.

It was a gift no one else in all the world, B.C. or A.D., could ever give. It was a gift from the heart of Jesus for the hearts and minds of His grieving followers—and for you and me.

But a gift is not a gift until it is received.

It would seem that no one who is aware of Christ's legacy to His own would be so foolish as not to claim it. There are cases on record when the beneficiary of a will has scorned to take advantage of it. And unquestionably, there are believers in Christ who have never availed themselves of the gift He left us.

When we *have* received our legacy, when we experience this "peace that passes understanding," as Paul phrases it, we can live with turmoil all around us and still have an untroubled heart, for the text of Christ's will reads, "Let not your heart be troubled, neither let it be afraid."

Aren't you glad you are one of our Lord's beneficiaries?

SHE DIDN'T KNOW GOD
ANSWERS PRAYER!

BIBLE READING: Psalm 34:1-8

Let us exalt his name together (v. 3*b*).

The young wife of a ministerial student was giving her personal testimony. She explained that both she and her husband had been Christians for just two years. Now, because of what this meant in their own lives, they had scrapped their earlier plans and with their three children had left the security of their home and business to train for Christian service.

"I had a problem that was really troubling me," she related, "and a Christian neighbor said she would pray about it. Well, I had always sort of believed in Jesus, but I didn't know He answered people's prayers!"

This discovery led to her conversion and her husband's.

People who have been raised in a Christian home or who have had Christian teaching all their lives can't begin to understand what it is to live without praying about everything and expecting the Lord to answer and to move into the situation. So, possibly one of the most effective tools for evangelism of our own neighbors is simply sharing with them this truth: God does hear and He does answer prayer. To many of them it will appear to be a whole new dimension of help to make living tolerable, for some of your neighbors and mine are about at the end of their resources. Telling them of God's offer, "Call upon me and I will answer," (Psalm 91:15) might come to some as a rope to a drowning man.

For it is all too true that, like the young ministerial student's wife, there are people who have some knowledge and a kind of belief in Jesus, but they have never had a personal experience with Him. They don't know that He is a Saviour who cares for His own *in this life* as well as in the next.

It may be that we need to be alert to our neighbor's troubles, then be quick to help them find the Specialist who invites heavy-laden people to come unto Him and find rest and relief—and *redemption* (Matthew 11:28).

THE COMING NEW WORLD

BIBLE READING: Revelation 21:1-8

Go home to thy friends and tell them (Mark 5:19).

A "Third World"—a "Fourth World." Both theologians and statesmen are tossing the terms around. Most of us don't even pretend to understand the ramifications of their third and fourth worlds.

But, as Hal Lindsay reminds us in the title of his latest book, there's a new world coming.

This new world is, of course, the "world" that John the apostle envisioned in his exile on Patmos. And whatever our views on prophecy, relentlessly, day by day, history moves toward its climax for the Christian—the second coming of our Lord and the events that will surround it.

What does it do to you when you think of your neighbor who will not be a part of the good things that are in store for us as believers? Of the neighbor for whom the blessed hope has no meaning and for whom only an eternity apart from God looms.

Maybe we need to remind ourselves that there is a third world—or a fourth or a fifth—that is the world of our unsaved neighbors. And one day the Lord may ask, "Why did you not tell your friends, your neighbors?" Will we answer, "But they had their chance. They had radio and TV; they could buy a Bible even in the supermarket or the drugstore. And with a church on every corner, Lord—"

In such ways we excuse ourselves here and now. But will our excuses stand up when we appear before the Lord?

There is one school of thought concerning evangelism that says, "No matter what else you do (pray, give to foreign missions, teach Sunday School, counsel at crusades, etc., etc.), you are failing to carry out Christ's commission (Acts 1:8) unless you are going to your own neighbors with the message of the gospel.

And what a joy is ours when we do win our neighbor to Jesus Christ, when we help them to be ready for the new world that's coming.

THE GOD WHO IS THERE

BIBLE READING: Psalm 125

The Lord is round about His people (v. 2).

Some of us who can scarcely name two mountains in other countries can rattle off the names of mountains in the Bible: Mt. Sinai, Mt. Hermon, Mt. Carmel, and a number of others. That's because many significant things in the Scriptures occurred on mountain tops, and we have become familiar with these mountains.

Mountains speak to us of endurance, strength, stability, majesty.

The psalmist had an affinity with mountains, and in them he saw some of the characteristics of God. In Psalm 36:6 he likens God's *righteousness* to the great mountains. Psalm 125 carries another heartening truth: "As the mountains are round about Jerusalem, so the Lord is round about his people from henceforth even for ever."

What does it mean to have Someone strong and enduring around us? It spells protection, security; more than that, it means freedom from devastating loneliness, often called the sickness of our times. No Christian living in daily fellowship with the Lord need feel unprotected, insecure, or all alone.

Often, people who live in proximity to mountains cannot see them. Clouds and fog and smog blot them from their view. Living as I do in Pasadena, California, I am keenly aware of this fact. Days, sometimes a week or more, can go by without there being even an outline of a mountain range on the horizon. Then with an atmospheric change, the mountains stand out clearly and majestically to bless our eyes and our souls. But they've been there all the time!

Sometimes clouds of grief or the smog of doubt may temporarily appear to blot God from our view. But God is there "from henceforth even for ever more." Anna Waring's hymn, "In Heavenly Love Abiding" poses this thoughtful question: "But God is round about me—and can I be dismayed?"

We can be, we are, at times dismayed. Perhaps, like David, we need to lift up our eyes "unto the hills"—and beyond, to the God Who is always *there*.

LET US DO SOMETHING

BIBLE READING: James 1:22-27

If a person just listens and doesn't obey (v. 23, TLB).

One of the national service organizations, the Jaycees, has as its motto: Do Something. As Christians we can be in hearty accord with them in their aim, for we, too, have a mandate to do something. James spells it out for us so that, whatever version we may like, the fact still stands out: "Dear brothers, what's the use of saying that you have faith and are Christians if you aren't proving it by helping others?" (2:14, TLB).

Nowhere is this more important than in our contacts with our unsaved neighbors. How often it is the practical demonstration of Christian love—*when this is done to help the person and not to bribe her to come to church*—that opens the door for later sharing our faith with this neighbor.

Many of us have had long and constant conditioning against "works," against anything that might be construed as "the social gospel." Consequently, we might stand indicted as being hearers of the Word and not doers, as being guilty of a lack of human compassion for the needy.

No one could ever accuse Jesus of such imbalance. He came to seek and to save that which was lost. And along the way, He saw and met human need. Yet we, His followers, often have a distorted view of what following Him entails. Jesus is the all-time Good Samaritan. He saw the need, and regardless of the person's condition or race or creed, He stepped in and helped, in a practical way, with the specific help that was needed.

It may be that our gospel message might have a hollow ring in the ears of some neighbor of ours: a neighbor who is plagued by human need of bread, next month's rent, or just a loving word and a pleasant greeting as she carries a heavy load about which we may not even know. James would say to us, "Do something. Don't just preach a sermon. Feed the hungry bodies before you attempt to unlock their hearts and minds to the Gospel."

How about it, neighbors? Let's do something, shall we— today?

GETTING BACK JUST WHAT YOU GIVE

BIBLE READING: Romans 12:14-21

If it be possible . . . live peaceably with all men (v. 18).

A preacher used to quip, "The Bible says, 'Live peaceably with all men—and some women.'"

There are some women who make people feel like that, as though you can scarcely live with them. We meet them in many everyday situations. I recall a waitress in a restaurant where a friend and I frequently had lunch. This waitress was almost impossible. She treated her customers as though she wished they had stayed home, almost threw the menu at us, and, in general, did a good job of alienating people.

At first, my friend Ruth, and I thought we would avoid her by going to another area of the coffee shop. But then we thought it over and decided she was a challenge. The food was good; so we had nothing to lose. We deliberately sat where she would be our waitress. We smiled at her and commiserated with her on how busy she was. We told her not to rush; we could wait. We left a generous tip each time, continued to smile, and to compliment her on her service to us as it began to improve. We never grumbled.

Gradually, she began to react to this treatment. She smiled at *us* and at her other customers, and she began to get good reactions from them, too. Because she began to seem happier than before, people gravitated to where she would serve them. It was a chain reaction. We had helped bring out the best in her.

We got just what we gave.

The same can work wonders with neighbors. How they act is their concern; how we react to their actions is ours.

It may take extra prayer for daily grace to put up with some neighbors and their foibles, even their nasty behavior toward us. But isn't that what God's grace is for? To provide us with the power *not* to retaliate, not to avenge ourselves? Moreover, it is a strict command of Scripture, "Recompense to no man evil for evil" (Romans 12:17).

There's great inner satisfaction in not "getting even" with people. It's for our own blessing as much as the other person's that God requires us to live peaceably with all men. For we get back just what we give.

WHAT ARE YOU LOOKING FOR?

BIBLE READING: Titus 2:11-15

We look for the Saviour (Philippians 3:20).

Have you known people who say, "I'm not one of those Christians who's always talking about the Lord's return. I'm not looking for the Lord's coming; I'm just living by His Word"?

It's commendable, of course, to live by the Christian's manual, the Bible. But, doesn't the Bible instruct us to be looking for the Lord's return? My Bible does. I read in Hebrews 9:28, "Unto them that look for him shall he appear the second time."

"Looking for Jesus" is not a matter of donning a white robe and sitting on a hilltop staring up at the sky. Some have done this, bringing the truth of Christ's return into disrepute through the years. Looking for Jesus is a *heart watch* while we work to redeem the time.

What does this "looking for the Lord's return" do for us? First, as John tells us in his first epistle (1 John 3:3), *it purifies us*. This ties in with what the book of Titus says about looking for that blessed hope (Titus 2:13). It causes us to live a godly life.

63

Second, it gives us an optimistic outlook on life, for our future is assured. This is in contrast with many of our neighbors who have nothing but the daily news to live by. No wonder they are pessimistic!

Third, looking for Jesus to come back for us gives a keen edge to our witnessing. I should know! It was when I heard *for the first time in my nineteen years* that Jesus Christ was coming back again that I listened to an evangelist. I was hooked by the fantastic story and thereby heard the gospel and believed and received Jesus as my Saviour. I wasn't about to lose out on such a tremendous opportunity!

There never was a better time to reach our neighbors. Many of them are already convinced by world conditions that "something has to happen." And we know the secret they need to know if they're going to be a part of the joy of the Lord's second coming.

So, while we live by God's Word, let's keep looking for our Lord—and keep helping other people to be ready when He comes.

PEOPLE ARE FOR APPRECIATING

BIBLE READING: Ephesians 2:8-13

We are his people (Psalm 100:3).

One of the glories of Christianity is that each individual is important for himself, not for what he *does*, but for what he *is*. Many a person goes throughout life without quite understanding this. Perhaps from childhood they have observed something like the following situation.

Mother is trying to do a job she finds too much for her, maybe hanging a picture or curtains. She says in the child's hearing, "I wish your Dad were home. I could use him right now." Or it may be that you, yourself, have said, "On

Saturday the neighbor's kid'll be home. I can use him."
(Remember, some pages back we determined that the neighbor's kid is a neighbor, too. Neighbors come in all sizes.)

We don't really mean "use" in the sense that we use a tool, a paint brush, or a vacuum cleaner. But it comes across to another person as if we mean it that way. And it is demeaning. We are indebted to child psychologist Heim Ginott for the statement in *Between Parent and Child:* "Things are for using; people are for loving."

What we are usually intending to say is, "I would appreciate having your Dad's help: his ability or strength or height or whatever the particular job called for. We use the strength or skill, not the person himself. We do not "use" a husband or son or brother or kindly neighbor.

That's nit-picking with words, you may be thinking. Maybe so. Nevertheless, none of us wants to have it said that someone is using us.

Children brought up hearing this frequently have trouble realizing that God loves them for themselves, that they do not have to prove anything to get God's favor, that they cannot work to gain salvation.

We do people a genuine service when we say to them *often,* "I appreciate you," not, "I appreciate what you just did." It's all right to say that, too; but we need to let people know that it is they themselves, not what they have done for us, that we appreciate most. Telling them this makes it easier for them to comprehend when we share with them the facts that God loves us and that Jesus died for us, no matter what we can or cannot do.

WHOSE WILL THE THINGS BE?

BIBLE READING: Luke 12:15-21

Lay up . . . treasures in heaven (Matthew 6:20).

There's a message for us as Christians in this parable that Jesus told (though we generally hear it applied to the unsaved where it has an indisputable impact). It can act as a *stop, look,* and *listen* sign, when we're dazzled by alluring ads for things and more things. It can cause us to ask, "Whose will all my things be?"

It's not that possessions are wrong in themselves. Certainly Jesus did not go around lecturing His followers on the sinfulness of legitimate needs. And everything in nature tells us that God wants us to appreciate beauty in this life. It's not the possession *of,* but the obsession *with* things that God deplores.

Frankly, wouldn't you agree that there should be a difference between the one whose goal is heaven and those who just live for this world? This difference should show up in our attitude toward things, on how much grip they have on us. For example, I know of a woman who told the evangelist holding revival meetings in her church, "I'm just miserable when you keep telling us the Lord may come soon. I don't want Him to come. Bob and I have scrimped and saved to build a new house. Now that we're just beginning to enjoy it, *I don't want the Lord to come soon.*" At least she was honest, this woman who really is a believer and who works diligently in her church. But she has balanced the glories of the second coming of Christ against her earthly home—and the scale weighed in favor of her house. No wonder she was miserable. God who made us knows that the excessive acquiring of worldly possessions, no matter how fine, can never bring inner peace. In fact, they more often destroy peace.

Not only is this tragic for the Christian; it presents a

distorted image to our unsaved neighbors. They see us getting our satisfaction from the same source as they themselves. This must be disillusioning to them, for their hearts, too, must hunger for a satisfaction that things have not brought them.

So perhaps we should say to ourselves quite frequently, "Am I laying up treasures in heaven?" We will never have to wonder whose things these will be.

IF THEY WOULD ONLY CHANGE

BIBLE READING: Revelation 1:1-6

Unto him that loved us, and washed us (v. 5).

A Christian woman complained to her husband, "If only Mary [her next-door neighbor] would *change*, there might be some hope for her!"

This woman had been diligently attempting to witness to her neighbor, Mary, without much apparent success; and the problem as she saw it was that the neighbor needed to change; then the Gospel would penetrate her thinking.

We may not admit it, but most of us at some time would like to change somebody. And if we could, it often might be an improvement. But this was not the issue in the case of Mary and her Christian neighbor. Think! How much did you have to change before the Lord reached out and saved you? How much did I change?

Christ loved us and washed away our sins in His own blood, the Bible tells us. He *loved* us—and *washed* us. In that order. Therein came the great change. God accepted us into His family as we were. We would never have been able to "shape up" enough to be acceptable to Him. But Jesus did the "shaping up" for us. It's good to keep this crystal clear in our own minds, or we may fall into the "works" trap. No amount of pulling up the bootstraps will impress God. He made the only effective provision for cleaning us up and fitting us for His presence.

It is not that there is anything wrong with viewing our neighbors and thinking, *What a change it would make in their lives if they were Christians!* But we need to keep two things in mind: (1) that our motive is pure, we want this good thing to happen to them *for their sakes* because we can't bear to know that they are lost; and (2) that we can best activate our longing for their salvation by our fervent prayer for them, prayer that by His Holy Spirit the Lord will convict and convert them. Then, often, the Lord graciously lets us have a part with Him in changing our neighbors (even as He is changing us daily).

We can help a new Christian—but Christ alone can change His children into His image.

THE GOD OF ALL COMFORT

BIBLE READING: 2 Corinthians 1:1-4

I will not leave you comfortless (John 14:18).

God must know that we need some things more than others, and He mercifully sees to it that we are not left deprived of these basic needs.

Comfort is high on the priority list. *"Comfort."* Even in the saying of this word, we can visualize warmth and love and understanding; and undoubtedly, to our mind comes someone who personifies these wonderful things for us.

Jesus was ever mindful of our human need for comfort. He, Himself, had been the comforter for His followers. But the day came when He was about to leave them. We can imagine the looks of dismay, of sorrow on their faces, looks that must have conveyed, "Who will comfort us when You are gone?" From that day until this, the words of Jesus have been the stay of countless millions: "I will not leave you comfortless." He told His disciples this—and you and me.

Our Lord kept His Word. He did send another Comforter, the Holy Spirit, to abide with us always.

Paul speaks of still another source of comfort for the believer," [The] comfort of the Scriptures" (Romans 15:4).

Is all this comfort just for ourselves, so that we can feel loved and wanted, so that we can revel in its warmth? Oh, no! I was impressed afresh as I read (speaking of the Holy Spirit) "whom the world cannot receive, because it seeth Him not, neither knoweth Him; but you know Him" (John 14:17).

In a world of trouble and sorrow and confusion and uncertainty, how do people keep their balance when they do not know the Lord, do not have the comfort of God's Holy Spirit, the guidance from His Word? Well might we ask ourselves this question. For we are not given all these blessings to hoard to ourselves. As we read in 1 Corinthians 1, God comforts us; but the comfort has a secondary purpose: that we might comfort them which are *in any trouble.*

Can you think of a better way to befriend your neighbor? And have you ever had a neighbor who never had any trouble?

KEEPING A SHORT ACCOUNT

BIBLE READING: Matthew 5:20-24

If, . . . you remember a friend has something against you (v. 23, TLB).

Can good things come out of war? Yes, sometimes.

My daughter, a missionary nurse in Bangladesh, tells of some moving things that happened among the Christians during the year of horror that preceeded the birth of Bangladesh.

"The pettiness was gone. People were loving and kind and thoughtful toward each other (missionaries and national Christians alike). We all lived with the knowledge that each time we met together could be the last time; with bombs raining down it was a realistic assumption. It was beautiful the way one would go to another and say, 'I want you to forgive me for—'; or 'If I've done or said anything to hurt you or offend you, will you forgive me?' None of us wanted to part with anything but love between us."

Sometimes it takes an extremity to remind us to keep a short account.

What happens when we do not, when we let things fester between another Christian and ourselves? (You may have read my *Christ For Everyday.* If so, you may recall this thought: *The person whom you cannot [or do not] forgive haunts your prayer life.*) This truth is inherent in our Scripture for today. This is the picture. You're on your knees with your gift of worship and praise when the Holy Spirit brings to your remembrance something rankling between you and another member of the Body of Christ. When this happens—*no matter whose fault it is*—the thing for you to do is get up, make a move, "pick up your gift," and go to the person. Clear the spiritual and emotional air—then return to pray and praise. This will keep your account short with your fellow Christians. (James 5:16 is an excellent formula.)

1 John 1:9 is the formula for keeping a short account with *God.*

"Confession is good for the soul," quips both Christian and non-Christian. And this is true. But confession is also good for one's peace of mind and for maintaining good relationships with other people. We are not in imminent danger of our lives as are some believers today, but it pays to keep a short account with God and with His people.

NOT MANNA AGAIN!

BIBLE READING: Exodus 16:4-8

Our soul loatheth this light bread (Numbers 21:5).

Does your family come to the table, look over the fare, then grumble, "Not hamburger again!" or, "Not left-over roast beef!" Or it may be meat loaf or chicken at which they are turning up their noses.

If you've had this experience a number of times, you can sympathize to some extent with Moses. In effect, the Israelites were saying, "Lord, You rescued us from slavery in Egypt. Big deal. There we at least had a variety of food. We had all the bread we could eat."

God dealt graciously with them. He said, "I'll rain down bread from heaven for you." (Note that it was not for everybody under the sun, just for the grumbling Israelites.) Were they thankful? Not particularly. At first they showed curiosity concerning "the bread from heaven," but later they griped, "Our soul loathes this light bread." (They wanted dark rye or pumpernickel?)

Moses struck at the root of the matter when he said of their complaining, "Your murmurings are not against us [Moses and Aaron] but against the Lord."

Innate in all of their murmuring, as in ours, was a lack of thankfulness for God's mercies. When we complain of sameness, "hamburger again," we are questioning God's goodness to us. It's as though we are saying, "God, can you not think of a new mercy to send me today? I know your mercies are new every morning, but can't You be a little creative and original day by day?" If this has an irreverent ring, how reverent does our complaining sound to God, I wonder.

But we need not be whiners, murmurers. We can find something for which to be thankful to God, something that will make us wake up expecting some good thing from God. Certainly He does not owe us anything, for the Bible says: "It is of the Lord's mercies that we are not consumed, because his compassions fail not. They are new every morning. Great is thy faithfulness" (Lamentations 3:22, 23).

That should be enough to stop even the chronic complainer, don't you think?

IT IS TIME TO DO IT

BIBLE READING: 1 Chronicles 28:2-6

Be strong, and do it (v. 10).

It had been a life dream of King David that he would build "a house for the Lord." When this privilege was denied him, he might have had a dog-in-the-manger attitude. But not David! It was more important to him that the temple be built than that he get the credit for building it.

In this chapter of Chronicles he is giving a pep talk to his son, Solomon, who is granted the privilege by God. David outlines for Solomon the design and encourages him with details of the materials on hand and the workman for each phase of the job; then he nails his son's assignment down with his terse, "Be strong and do it," underscoring his command in the twentieth verse, where he indicates the need for courage in getting the work done.

Solomon had not sought the illustrious task of building a temple. But when God assigned him the job, God saw to it that everything necessary for the building was provided.

It should encourage us when God calls us to a particular task, whether it's something we have dreamed of doing for Him or not, that with the assignment comes the enabling. What we set out to do may seem to other people to be too much for us, or it may appear to be our own "impossible dream." No matter. If we're sure God is leading us to do it, He will make it possible for us to accomplish the goal.

A few days ago, a student in the Rosemead Graduate School of Psychology stepped into my office. His face was shining. He works with a community group—purely secular—as their chaplain, *at their request.* And God had just shown this bright young man an ambitious plan for reaching not only the immediate community but also a broad segment of our country. "It's *big,*" he said to me, "and I want you to pray with me. I believe the Lord wants me to do something about it." (He had already begun.)

When you're sure of what God wants you to do, *go and do it*, in spite of all obstacles.

HOW DO YOU KNOW YOU HAVE FAITH?

BIBLE READING: Hebrews 11:23-30

The trying of your faith worketh patience (James 1:3).

"I've been doing my congregation an injustice," a pastor admitted. "I have failed to help them to see God's purposes in permitting suffering."

No wonder we shake our heads and sigh about "our faith being tried" when some sorrow comes our way. And yet, how else do we know we have faith or how strong our faith really is?

Suffering, in one form or another (physical, emotional, mental, or even financial) can be God's way of letting us find out if, indeed, we do have faith in Him, faith in His loving willingness to care for us, faith in His ability to do what is best for us.

That tow rope lying in the garage or the car trunk may look stout and reliable. But comes the day when you need it, and—ee—its strands split apart. It can't stand the test.

Because God loves us and has a plan for our lives, He tests us from time to time. But never will He test us beyond our ability to bear the test. The Lord has clearly promised this (1 Corinthians 10:13). God's honor is at stake. He will keep His Word to His children.

It pays to regard trouble and trials as Paul did. "Our light afflictions [surely an understatement!] work for us" (2 Corinthians 4:17). It's as though, recognizing God's intent in permitting trials to come upon him, Paul dared—*challenged*—these trials to get him down.

Not always will we know the reason why suffering comes our way. But we are frequently allowed to see the results, *if we accept the trial as from the Lord* and look for His hand in it. Time and time again, the patient trust of a Christian passing through a severe trial is the one thing that has spoken to her neighbors. They have recognized a power to "take trouble," and they have been forced to the conclusion that the Christian has, as one woman put it, "outside help." (Actually, as we know, it's *inside* help.)

This testimony can result only when we pass the faith test.

THE UTTERMOST PARTS NEXT DOOR

BIBLE READING: Acts 1:1-8

You will receive power to testify about me with great effect (v. 8, TLB).

Lucy had always been interested in missions and missionaries. Her strong desire had long been to reach someone for the Lord in an "uttermost part of the earth." But her life had not moved in that direction.

Going about her housework one Monday, she kept hearing something the junior church children had sung the day before about God sending them across the street or across the sea.

Later, as she tuned in the Christian radio station, the speaker was saying, "We can't all go to the far places of the earth. But we can all go to the nearest place to us, with the Gospel message."

Lucy had heard that before. It did not move her. She wanted God to use her in a more glamorous way than that. But the Holy Spirit would not let her dismiss the Scriptural injunction that easily. The instruction is to witness at "Jerusalem" (right where we are) as well as the more distant places.

You would really have to hear Lucy tell it herself to get the full impact of how God gave her this desire and yet let her fulfill her dream.

"I felt uneasy about not particularly wanting to witness to my neighbor," she admits. "Then I fancied myself setting off around the world to the uttermost part, traveling right around the globe to win someone for Christ. Suddenly it dawned on me that if I were to actually do this, the farthest place I would reach before returning to my home would be my next-door neighbor's! It didn't take me long to start witnessing to them, believe me! And the Lord graciously let me have a part in winning them to Himself."

Isn't that a fantastic thought? We each have an "uttermost-part" neighbor! Our Jerusalem can be our own block, our own street.

And what is "witnessing"? Just telling our own experiences. Nothing is half so effective in evangelism as to share what Christ has done in our own lives. How about sharing, this very day, with your uttermost-part neighbor?

HOW TO COPE

As thy days, so shall thy strength be (Deuteronomy 33:25).

"The single greatest problem of my women readers," stated a newspaper columnist, "is coping."

Coping is a catchall word for our times, meaning different things to different people. To some it connotes managing under the circumstances; to others, it is barely keeping their heads above water. And how often we hear, "I just can't cope."

God has provided a formula for coping.

"As thy days, so shall thy strength be," the Bible says. This is a great stabilizer for the emotions, for the times when we feel, *I have so much to do. I'll never get it all done.*

Think of the nights when you have looked back at the duties of the day and sighed, *I could never do it all over.* That's the right way to feel at night, for you have used up your promised strength for the day. We're given enough: no more, no less. And we would borrow on tomorrow's allotted portion at peril to our physical and emotional health. Tomorrow's strength is for tomorrow's needs. If we could mortgage it, how would we repay it?

When we're living close to the Lord, seeking His guidance day by day, striving to live fruitful Christian lives, we will always have strength to do what God wants us to do. It's not a matter of coping, or we would all be saying, "I can't cope." It's a matter of depending on God's promise.

And isn't it wonderful that God does not let time be a great unbroken expanse. In His wisdom and love He slices it into day and night. He gives strength for the day and rest for the night. Not like a prescription to be taken at will, does God dispense strength. He renews us daily. We can neither recapture yesterday's strength nor dissipate tomorrow's. As we sometimes sing in "He Giveth More Grace" by Annie Johnson Flint,

> He giveth more grace when the burden grows
> greater;
> He giveth more strength when the labors increase.

This is scripturally sound. It makes it possible for you and me to cope.

BUT IT TAKES FOREVER

BIBLE READING: Matthew 6:27-34

My times are in thy hand (Psalm 31:15A).

A young woman said so wistfully, "Everything I want takes forever." There was a world of hurt and longing in her voice.

I admit to having thought the same as she, more than once. I vividly recall my grandmother's comment when I would daydream about the future and wish out loud that time would hurry up. "You're just wishing your life away, child," she would say. It took a long time for her wisdom to make sense to me.

It's normal, however, for children to have such feelings.

Teenagers, too, become frustrated because it seems to them that what they most desire "takes forever."

It's a mark of maturity, then—an indication that we have grown up to a certain extent—when we no longer become annoyed at having to wait for the fulfillment of our desires.

More than that, it's a measure of our spiritual growth.

Actually, when we think it through, we can see that always wanting what we don't have and being impatient about it, says, "I'm not satisfied with my present. I want what the future has in store for me." Inherent in this attitude is our dissatisfaction with what God is doing in our lives today.

When we can grow beyond this childish stage, we're so much happier and contented and at peace with ourselves and other people. We accept each day as a gift from God; we thank Him for it and recognize our stewardship for its hours.

In a different context Jesus said, "Take no thought for tomorrow." But can we apply it to this situation? Our times—our day-by-day-life—are in His hands. Why then should we fret and be discontented and think, "Everything I want takes forever"?

With a right attitude toward today, we may even hasten the fulfillment of our dreams for tomorrow.

GOD IS NOT ASKING YOU TO TAKE ON THE WORLD

BIBLE READING: Philippians 3:7-14

One thing I do (v. 13).

If you are like me, you're sometimes overwhelmed by all there is to do. At such times we follow one of two courses open to us.

One, we dwell on "all there is to do" and get tired just thinking about it. We then tend to rationalize, "I'm just one person. I can't be expected to do everything." The next thought can logically be, *Why try? What difference will my little contribution make?* So we fail to do the one (or two or three) thing we *can* do. This robs us of a feeling of fulfillment and also throws an added burden on other people who then have to do these things.

Two, we tackle a pile of things, and from sheer lack of

hours and limited energy, some of these tasks are left half-done. In some instances it would have been better if they had not been started.

Either option brings frustration. What, then, is the solution of the too-busy program?

Paul found the answer. He had his "thing": his "one thing." Certainly Paul had more than one area of activity; he preached, taught, traveled, wrote, to name a few; but each one fed into his total goal: "Pressing on to the mark of the prize of his high calling." Paul worked at his trade, along the way, to support himself, but whatever he gave himself to was always with his ultimate aim in view. In this, he can be an excellent example for all of us.

For the committed Christian, the supreme goal ought to be, "How can I *best* serve the Lord in the circumstances in which He has placed me *today?*"

We may at times have to close our ears to the suggestions and ideas of other people concerning how we can accomplish our goal. For God is not asking us to take on the world, to meet every need, to work at every project about which we hear. But He *is* expecting us to do something to make an impact on our unsaved neighbors.

To relieve our frustration over "all there is to do" and to achieve our goal of doing our "one thing," let's ask *God* to direct us. Pray, "Lord, what will YOU have me to do today?" Then let's enjoy His peace as we go ahead and do it.

WHEN WE OVERSTAY OUR WELCOME

BIBLE READING: Proverbs 25:11-17

Be ye . . . wise as serpents (Matthew 10:16).

The Bible is the most practical of books, and poet and

songwriter though he was, King Solomon shows real insight into the problems of everyday living. Chapter 25 zeros in on a number of pertinent issues, for example, being sensitive in our relationships with our neighbors.

"Let your foot rarely be in your neighbor's house, lest he become weary of you and hate you" (v. 17, Berkeley).

This might sound contrary to 2 Timothy 4:2, "Be instant in season, and out of season" (which is equally important). However, the Lord Jesus Christ gave a directive in Matthew 10:16 that applies in both instances. "Be wise as serpents and harmless as doves," He counseled.

How does this apply spiritually to "Letting your foot be rarely in your neighbor's house"? Let me illustrate: Just a week ago I met a keen Christian couple. They had been saved just a few months and are fervent witnesses. The Lord is blessing them, and a number of their associates have come to Christ.

"My husband never gives up," the wife told me with a little smile; then she added, "but I think he might get farther with our neighbors if he would ease up a little, let them have some time to think about what he's said—Oh, I'm not complaining," she was quick to explain. She undoubtedly didn't realize she was echoing Solomon's words when she went on to say, "It's just that I'm afraid they might get to hate the sight of us."

It would not be the Christian couple themselves that the unsaved neighbors would "hate the sight of"; it would be all they stand for, their faith in Jesus Christ, their belief in God.

But can any of us afford to alienate even one neighbor by not being wise as serpents? By, in a sense, overstaying our welcome? There are ways to witness and a time for everything (Ecclesiastes 3:1). The Holy Spirit will guide us as we seek to encourage our neighbors to taste and see that the Lord is good; then He will do the work in their hearts without our overstaying our welcome.

DON'T SAVE IT—GIVE IT AWAY

BIBLE READING: Ephesians 5:15-20

Wise people who make the best possible use of their time (v. 15-16, Berkeley).

Isn't it nice to have someone say, "Thank you for the time you spent with me" or "I knew it took your time, and I appreciate it"?

Conversely, some people complain, "She took *so much* of my time!" And there is a built-in "How could she?" in the person's voice.

What are they saying, both the grateful and the gripers? That *time* is our great possession and that most people like to keep it. We are not too much unlike Napoleon who selfishly, but perhaps more honestly than many of us, said "Ask me for anything but my time."

Time is a solemn trust, and we do well to guard it.

"Time" also provides us with our prime excuse: "I'd like to—but I don't have the time," we tell ourselves and other people.

What if God had no time for us! Perhaps one of our greatest sources of security as believers is that God does have time for us. We don't have to seek an appointment, arrive on the dot, and be ushered out when our time is up.

God has given us our allotted time, and we are exhorted to "redeem it." Each of us has the same number of minutes in an hour and hours in our days. How do we "make the best possible use of our time"? Buy opportunities with it. Share it with someone who needs us. The need for help is always all around us. We would gladly give our abilities, our skills, our energy and—usually—our money. What keeps us from always being the good neighbor we might be? *It takes our time.* Nothing—*nothing* can ever be accomplished without someone's giving up time.

"Life's too short," we often say in justification of what

we don't do. We are indebted to Victor Hugo for this piece of wisdom: "Short as life is, we make it still shorter by the careless waste of time." True, we do not want to waste one minute. Nor should we want to hoard our minutes. So—let's not save our time. Let's give it away!

GETTING DOWN TO BASICS

BIBLE READING: Hebrews 5:13-14; Joshua 1:8

Thou shalt meditate therein (Joshua 1:8).

We are living in a health-conscious culture. The merits of jogging, nutrition, and kindred subjects monopolize many a conversation. These deal with two of the generally accepted three basic ingredients of normal health: food and exercise.

Thinking about this one day recently, I simply could not call to mind the third one. Suddenly it dawned on me: *rest.* (Later, honesty made me admit that, undoubtedly, the reason I "forgot" number three was that rest has not been sufficiently important to me. I am remedying this, however, because for true balance we need all three: food, exercise, and rest.)

The spiritual analogy immediately comes to mind.

Food. We enter God's family as we enter our natural family, as babies. In order to grow and mature we need food, first "the milk of the Word" and later, "strong meat." It saddened Paul to find certain Christians remaining bottle babies (1 Corinthians 3:1, 2), with the attendant problems this created.

Exercise. When our intake exceeds our body's ability to assimilate, certain disorders result. So it is in the spiritual realm. The Christians who run from Bible conference to prophetic conference all the time, without giving out as much as they absorb, begin to develop a kind of nit-picking, critical attitude toward other believers. They may be suffering from spiritual indigestion, from too much food and too little spiritual exercise. In addition, they lose out on the joy of *service* for the Lord.

Rest. As our body demands rest if it is to function well, so our spirit; our soul needs periods of rest. We need *planned times* to get away from our routine (or rat race) in order to read God's Word, to be quiet before Him, to meditate. The secular world is making much of meditation these days, meditation as a panacea for confusion of mind. But long ago, men of God recognized the worth of disciplined meditation. David makes mention of meditating day and night; Paul exhorts Timothy to meditate. This is the same command the Israelites were given by Joshua.

Food, exercise, rest—we need all three basics if we are going to be balanced, productive Christians. So, shall we get down to basics today?

YOU ARE NEVER TOO OLD TO GROW

BIBLE READING: Psalm 92:12-15

They shall still bring forth fruit in old age (v. 14).

We use the term "growing old," but all too often the two words contradict themselves in our thinking. In many circles the concept is that the older years are not a time for growth.

In our youth-emphasis culture, it's no wonder that the senior citizens downgrade their ability to be productive and to grow in many areas. But we all improve with encouragement as people express their belief in us.

A Sunday school teacher impressed on her class of older women the importance of memorizing Scripture.

"We're getting too old," they replied. But the teacher

did not give up. "Your memory isn't like the top drawer; holding just so much and no more," she encouraged them. "Let's learn verses together," and she outlined a realistic program.

Occasionally she got a little static: "We're too old." So she reminded them that the only people who were not getting old were already dead! This was a new thought to most of them, and it perked them up. Before long they were quoting whole sections of the Bible that they had memorized.

Some people are getting old.

Some are growing old.

Perhaps our modern society does not expect much from older people. But *God* does. In God's program the older years are productive years as we have read in Psalm 92. The condition is that the person belongs to the Lord. It's "the righteous who flourish and bring forth fruit in old age."

There's something wonderfully serene about a man or woman who has come to old age having known the Lord for a lifetime.

Contrast such a person with the one who is old and who does not know the Lord, who is just *getting* older while the Christian is *growing* older.

Since everyone of us, from the day we were born, has been on the road to old age, it would be good to stop and evaluate, "Am I *growing* older, and along the way, am I bringing forth fruit?"

WHEN GOD SAYS "GO"

BIBLE READING: Ezekiel 3:16-19

A true witness delivereth souls (Proverbs 14:25).

Have you ever experienced an unusual leading to go to

84

witness to a particular person? If you have, you will understand why some people hang back, arguing with the Lord before obeying His strange direction.

Driving her children to school, a Christian woman observed a man working in his front yard, and day by day she had a growing conviction that the Lord wanted her to go to witness to this man.

For about a week she argued, "But, Lord, I don't know this person. He's not *my* neighbor? Why do you want *me* to go? What will I tell him is my reason for coming to his door?" But in spite of her reluctance, the feeling persisted. So she drove up to his house, got out of the car, and began to talk with him about his flowers and his shrubs and lawn. Then she steered the conversation around to her purpose in coming to see him.

"Oh, you're one of *those*," he sniffed, backing away from her. "Well, let me tell you that those others have come, stopping at every house on the street, peddling their propaganda, but they never get to me!"

Quietly she said, "But I'm not like the others. I didn't stop at any house but yours. *God* sent me, and He just sent me to your house to talk with you."

He blinked, incredulous at what she was saying. "You mean," he gasped, "that *God sent you to talk to me*, not to my neighbors on this side or the other—just *me?*"

"That's right," she assured him.

Asked if he had a Bible, he replied that he did not; even if he had one he probably would not read it. "If I bring my Bible once a week, will you let me read it to you," she offered. And he took her up on it.

God honored her obedience, and the Holy Spirit began to work in the man's heart.

It was just a few weeks later, when this woman arranged for a pastor to call on the man, that he trusted Christ as his Saviour.

When God says "Go," it pays to heed if we don't want

someone's blood required of us and if we want to know the joy that inevitably follows obedience to God's leading.

THEY DID NOT HAVE A NEIGHBOR

BIBLE READING: Matthew 25:34-46

When did we ever see you . . . sick, and not help you? (v. 44, TLB).

It is an incredible story. But according to the *Los Angeles Times* (Oct. 2, 1973), two patients, ages fifty-four and sixty, sitting in an emergency room in Miami, Florida, died in their wheelchairs. And it was four hours before any of the busy nurses or physicians noticed.

Can there be a more graphic instance of, "When did we see you sick and not help you"?

We cannot know all the circumstances, nor would we indict the staff, who must have had sufficient reason for their apparent neglect; otherwise, it would surely be a matter of criminal neglect. But that such a thing could happen, this is the tragedy! *Someone* must have been neighbor to one or both of these dying persons.

Sometimes it takes such an extreme example of human desperation to cause us to look deep into our own hearts and see what is there. Would you—would I—ever be guilty of such inhumanity, such gross neglect of a sick neighbor if we knew about the need?

And, if we didn't know, what kind of neighbors are we?

It's clear that Jesus puts a high value on sick and suffering people. Matthew 25 makes it amply plain that there is commendation from the King Himself for the one who will show compassion to the needy. It is also plain that awful punishment is in store for those who disregard their fellow human beings who are in distress.

Where have we, as Christ's followers, gone off the track?

Why do so many of us either fail to read or deliberately refuse to heed such passages as we have in Matthew and again in James 2:15. And there is the good samaritan story.

There is still time for us to get on the King's *right* side. Today we can help somebody who needs help, and tomorrow and tomorrow. We *can* one day hear, "Come, ye blessed of my Father . . ." (Matthew 25:34).

THE CHOSEN ONES

BIBLE READING: John 15:9-16

You didn't choose me! I chose you (v. 16, TLB).

All of us, from early childhood, like to be chosen. We felt good when we were chosen on somebody's "side" for a game. We were proud to be selected by our teacher to do something, whether it was to clean the blackboard or take the lead part in a play. We were singled out, and this made us feel special.

As adults, while we might balk at working on a committee, we nevertheless like to be chosen for the position.

The first time I read John 15:16, I thought it was just for me. A new Christian, I was just following along as older believers guided me. "Read John's gospel," a lady had said, and she provided me with a Bible. I can still remember the morning this Bible fell open at John 15, and there leapt out at me, "Ye have not chosen me, but I have chosen you." The sheer truth of the words struck me. "That's true!" I said aloud. So I read on. I learned that not only had God chosen me (and it was quite a while before I considered that He had chosen other people, too), but that He had a *purpose*, a *plan* in doing so.

God's assignment for us is that we bear fruit. Did He mean the fruit of the spirit? Certainly this is a part of our ordained reason for being; this internal fruit has its effects, not only on our own lives but also on the lives of all whom we touch from day to day.

On the broader scene, the "fruit" will be those who, with the help of the Holy Spirit, will be our harvest of souls.

As the Lord has chosen us and planted us in different soil and in varying environments, so we will be able to bring forth fruit accordingly: you winning your neighbor; and I, mine. We may often feel rejected as we labor. And it is at such times we need to remind ourselves that we are specially chosen, we are God's ordained messenger. He has chosen us for His side. He has elected us to His committee. With this to spur us on, our thoughts should be of success as we witness, not failure. As God's chosen ones, we *can* go and we *can* exert an influence on others that will last through all eternity as "fruit that remains."

THE MAKING OF MEMORIES

BIBLE READING: Luke 16:22-31

Son, remember . . . (v. 25).

A lovely old song speaks with deep meaning in the line, "O memories that bless and burn!"

For memories *can* bless—and memories *do* come with scorching reminder of things we would fain forget.

All day long, wherever we are, whatever we are doing, each of us is in the memory-making process. We are causing the members of our own family and the little boy next door and the milkman and the mailman—anyone with whom we rub shoulders—to store up memories of us. Oh, they will not consciously be thinking, *I must remember how nice she was,* or *how brusque* or *how unthinking.* But all unbidden the impressions will be imprinted to be recalled perhaps days, perhaps years later.

It is an awesome thought that, according to science, everything we have ever heard or seen or felt is programmed into the marvellous computer that is our brain.

We need not rely on modern science for this knowledge, however. Our Lord Himself made it plain that memory lingers on even beyond the grave. (And, lest you're thinking, *But Jesus was speaking in parables*, surely you will agree that He would never teach other than the *truth*, either in direct speech or by a parable.)

"Son, remember," Jesus said. And it's plain that this man did remember. He had painful memories, memories of his brothers who, unless they would believe, would suffer the same fate as he.

We, too, will retain our ability to remember. So will those whose lot is cast with ours in this life. Their happiest remembrance of you or me will unquestionably be that we cared enough to tell them about Jesus, to warn them that there is, indeed, a heaven to gain and a hell to shun.

It's not too late for us to create these happiest of memories!

WHAT'S A NEIGHBOR FOR?

BIBLE READING: Matthew 19:19; Mark 12:31; Luke 10:27

Let us love, . . . in deed and in truth (1 John 3:18).

What's a neighbor for?

Our Lord Jesus Christ gave us the answer to that question!

A neighbor is for *loving*. In whatever gospel we read, it comes out the same: "Thou shalt love thy neighbor." Not only this, but also "Thou shalt love thy neighbor *as thyself*."

Perhaps we fail most in not living by the latter part of the verse. Long conditioning has caused many Christians to be hesitant to even *like* themselves, to say nothing of *loving* themselves. Is it any wonder that they have a hard time loving their neighbors!

Of course, Christ was speaking of a healthy love for oneself, not an inordinate, self-centered, "me first" attitude.

Why should we not think well of ourselves when God has made us what we are: His highest creation, made in His image? When we can "love ourselves" in this light, we are able to extend ourselves and love our neighbor.

This love which Jesus advocates for our neighbor is the kind that John writes about. It's not all talk, although talking, listening, just visiting together, and sharing our faith are vital parts of being a good neighbor. Sometimes the very kindest deed we can do is just to be there (with our soup or without) when a neighbor needs somebody with whom to talk.

We will have to do more than talk, however, to show the neighbor we love her. The love will make us sensitive to and aware of other needs. We will not foist ourselves on a neighbor at the wrong time, and we will not withhold our help at the right time.

What's a neighbor for? A neighbor is for loving and for showing that we love—by word and by deed.

WHEN WE LET GOD SPEAK

BIBLE READING: Isaiah 55:9-12

Comfort ye, comfort ye ... saith your God (Isaiah 40:1).

Have you gone to try to comfort a neighbor who was going through a severe trial but found yourself at a loss for the right words? I admit that this has happened to me. What can we do in such situations?

It was from a Christian doctor I learned a valuable lesson.

Chief of surgery at the world-famous City Of Hope, Dr. Ralph Byron is confronted daily with people of all races and creeds, the common denominator among them being that they are victims of cancer. As he makes his rounds and pauses by their beds, he many times lets God speak to them: "I don't change my voice, don't intone. I never say, 'Now, listen, for I'm going to quote some verses from the Bible,'" he relates, "but in a conversational voice, I repeat some well-known verse like 'The Lord is my shepherd; I shall not want' or 'I will never leave you or forsake you.' People recognize that the words are from the Bible—and God's Word itself has a calming effect on them."*

According to Dr. Byron, the greatest fear of the cancer patient is that their doctors will abandon them at some point, give up on them. So, when, in addition to reassuring them on this score, he lets God speak through His Word, the effect is significant. In fact, when this Christian physician deliberately fails to include something from the Bible in his conversation, a patient will frequently say, "Doctor, haven't you forgotten something?"

We, too, in our contacts with troubled people can let God speak. Like this busy doctor we will have to have committed some verses to memory so they are ready for such occasions. "What verses?" you may be asking. And that's a good question, for troubles vary and people are likewise different. It would seem to me that the verses which comfort you, yourself, are the best ones to use to help someone else—"The comfort wherewith we ourselves are comforted of God" (2 Corinthians 1:4).

Such comfort cannot fail to be effective, for God has said His Word *will* accomplish what He pleases—and it pleases God to comfort people.

*From Dr. Byron's commencement address at Rosemead Graduate School of Psychology, June 1973. Used by permission.

SAY IT WITH LOVE

BIBLE READING: Ephesians 4:11-15

Speaking the truth in love (v. 15).

"It's not what she said; it's how she said it."

How often do we hear someone say this, and nearly always with the complaint, we can sense a note of longing.

We can accept truth when it is mixed with love and concern.

I've heard some ministers quip about the woman who said, "My talent is *speaking my mind*," and they usually go on to tell their own response to such a person and her "talent": "That's a talent the Lord would have you *bury*." People generally laugh heartily at this point. But it's not all that funny.

God *has* given gifts for which we are accountable. But God has not given to any of us "the gift of speaking our mind" in the negative sense.

We do have a responsibility to speak the truth at all times. But it need not be barbed truth. It can be palatable, even as the worst tasting medicine is often sugar coated. It is possible for us to get across the point that a person is undoubtedly bound for hell unless he does something about it, unless he confesses his sins and accepts Christ's offer of eternal life. In addition, there are ways to show that we *care*, that we can't bear it that this person is not saved. Love is the factor that makes truth acceptable. Sometimes one neighbor has to make a justifiable complaint about another neighbor's child. Prefacing the complaint with, "I love your little girl and I'm sure there's likely a reason for (whatever she did)," will prevent defensive barriers being raised between the neighbors.

For the most part, we don't deliberately hurt one another by neglecting to speak the truth in love; we just don't realize how it sounds to the other person and what it will do to her. So, maybe we need to put the Golden Rule into practice: "As you would that your neighbor speak to you, so speak you to her" (if I may paraphrase it). This should guarantee that we speak the truth in love!

YOU CAN SCHEDULE YOUR WORRIES

BIBLE READING: Philippians 4:4-8

Get away from me, you Satan! (Matthew 16:23, TLB).

One of the reasons why we should not worry is that the Lord has exhorted us not to. "Be anxious for nothing," God's Word tells us.

There is a second reason why it pays to refuse to worry.

When worry comes in the door, creativity and initiative fly out the window. Why is this? When our minds are already filled to the choking point with worry—worry—worry, even the Holy Spirit cannot find room in our hearts and minds for inspiration. How can He place ideas into our consciousness which would then help us in the situation?

Most of the things we worry about are those about which we are powerless to do something. We are powerless except for one thing; we can *worry*.

I have found a working solution to this dilemma, and I am increasingly grateful that the Lord made this so clear to me. My friends smile when they hear me say, "I'll have to schedule that worry for later," but some of them have tried it and found it works.

Troubles come to me as they do to you. I used to fret and fume and fuss and complain to God and man. Now, with the insight the Holy Spirit has given me, I say when

I might be tempted to worry, "Get thee behind me, Satan," or as *The Living Bible* puts it, "Get away from me, you Satan! You are a dangerous trap to me. You are thinking merely from a human point of view, and not God's." Then I ask the Lord to help me keep my mind off such things because I cannot do anything about them. And I find that my day is not a dead loss as it would otherwise have been. It is good to commit our worries, our anxiety, and our fears—anything that would clutter up our mind with negative thinking—*early in the day*. Then we have the rest of the day for creative living. In the process we frequently find a way out of some problem rather than wallowing in thoughts of the problem itself.

By scheduling our worries until we have nothing else to think about, we may find we have scheduled them right out of existence. It's certainly worth a try, don't you agree?

SINGING CHRISTIANS

BIBLE READING: Colossians 3:12-17

Singing to the Lord with thankful hearts (v. 16, TLB).

It has been well said that Christianity is the only singing religion. Others have their music, but for the most part it sounds like a funeral dirge in minor key and mournful tones.

Undoubtedly such singing does not spring from a thankful heart.

But not only is singing good as an expression of our praise and gratitude to God; Paul exhorts us to "Remember what Christ taught and let His words enrich your lives and make you wise; teach them to each other and sing them out in psalms and hymns and spiritual songs" (v. 16, TLB).

Many of today's young people appear to have taken Paul seriously. They're singing their Gospel folk songs, and others are listening. For long years the arch enemy of Christianity, the forces of Communism, have drilled their young people through singing slogans propagating their doctrine.

It's interesting that "psalms" are mentioned as material for song. Actually there is no finer way to memorize a psalm than to sing it. (Who in Christian circles does not know Psalm 23? And many will testify to having unconsciously memorized it through singing it or hearing it sung.) Psalm 121 is the same: the beautiful "Unto the Hills" by Campbell comes from it.

We rob ourselves when we do not sing, whether we are crow or nightingale types.

We women, especially, can take to heart what some experts in the field are telling us: Singing is good as a preventative against wrinkles in the face.

And singing mothers make happy households. It's rather hard, for instance, for the mother in the home to snap at her child or at her husband or her neighbor, in the middle of "Tell Me the Old, Old Story" or some other heart-warming hymn. It is a favored family who starts the day by hearing Mom humming or singing in the kitchen as she prepares breakfast.

When God asks us to do something, we can be sure there are benefits in obeying. Not only is there the good feeling that we are obedient, but we have the special good that God intended when He issued the directive. God says "Sing!" We have plenty to sing about. So why not be a singing Christian today—and bless someone else and yourself, too.

BOTH YOURS AND MINE

I am the Good Shepherd and I recognize my own
(John 10:14, Berkeley).

You have probably been in a situation where someone, perhaps a neighbor or a relative, has talked about something that is exclusively hers. There is nothing wrong with such talk, unless of course, the purpose of it is to put down other people. This happens when one person boasts of family possessions as though no one else present could possibly own such things.

Actually we all like to have exclusive ownership of *something*. It's significant that among the first words a baby says are, "Me" and "Mine."

We tend to think of the personal pronoun as denoting selfishness. But that is not always so, or David the psalmist would be supremely selfish.

"The LORD is my Shepherd," he states with no smugness or apology. Then David makes great claims on the basis of this personal relationship. "I shall not lack," he declares, outlining all the areas of his life (and death): his good times and the days when enemies would surround him.

We're familiar with the words, with their beauty and simple grandeur.

But it's not enough to know the words, to be able to repeat the beloved Psalm 23. We have to appropriate its truth; we have to be "selfish" and grab onto that *my* Shepherd.

All the green pastures, all the peace and refreshment of the still waters, all the freedom from fear as we traverse the valley of the shadow, all the protection a shepherd affords each member of his flock—these and every other provision for peace of heart and soul and mind are reserved *exclusively* for those to whom the Lord is *"my Shepherd."*

The Shepherd Psalm offers continuing blessing: "all the days of my life." The Shepherd keeps eternal vigil (John 10:28-29).

Who is this Shepherd? Jesus answers the question of our hearts, "I am the Good Shepherd." He is *my* Shepherd, but you can make sure He is yours, too.

WHO SAYS SO?

BIBLE READING: Exodus 5:1-3

Who is the Lord, that I should pay attention to His orders (v. 2, Berkeley).

"Who says so?" Sometimes the question indicates resentment, sometimes rebellion; rarely is it a sincere bid for information. (It would be difficult to believe that the ruler of Egypt was ignorant as to who "the God of the Hebrews" was.) Rather, his question would indicate his utter disregard, even his contempt, for the God of Israel. Notice, also, that Pharaoh made no bones about the fact that whoever this God was, he was not going to obey Him. "I will not let Israel go," he stated.

Does this savor of some of your contacts with your unsaved neighbors?

In spite of all your efforts to share the Gospel with them, they have a "Who says so?" attitude. All too often, they too suggest that, even if they understood, they still would not pay much attention to what God says.

Generally it is futile to use our own arguments to try to convince them. We dead-end into a brick wall of unreasonable thinking, or prejudice.

A prominent Christian in Southern California, Benjamin Weiss, shared his experience with me. An ardent believer in soul-winning, he was not having too much success at first. Then an older, more experienced Christian worker gave him this wise counsel: "Don't argue from your own position of knowledge. *Use the Bible.*"

Mr. Weiss admits, "Until then, when I was dealing with a person about spiritual matters, it was just my word against his. But when I took this good advice and gave people what *God* said, oh, the difference that has made!" And for many years, Mr. Weiss, president of the National Educators Fellowship (an organization for Christian teachers in the public schools), has been noted for his success in soul-winning. Frequently he has been in charge of all the counselors at great Christian Crusades.

"Who says so?" Our answer can be "thus saith the Lord." Not too many will dare, like Pharaoh, to flout our God.

When, having given our neighbor something from God's Word, we can then authenticate it by saying, "I know it's true; it works for me," we have two factors going for us in our efforts to win this neighbor to Christ.

IN THE NAME OF JESUS

BIBLE READING: Acts 3:1-9

By what name, have ye done this? (Acts 4:7).

A Sunday school teacher told her class, "When we pray in the name of Jesus, it is like putting a stamp on a letter. The postage stamp assures delivery." This may be an oversimplified explanation, but it is worth considering.

We can never fathom the power of the name of Jesus, but we can be beneficiaries of this power. It's as though we possessed a royal seal which, when we make use of it, puts all the power of heaven at our disposal.

Wouldn't you like to have been there that day when Peter and John, worshipers on their way into the temple, paused by a lame beggar positioned at the Beautiful Gate? What thoughts raced through their minds? Did they, by a look at each other, communicate, "What would Jesus have done?" It's certain that they were not thinking that they had the power in themselves to heal (3:12).

Quickly they made it clear to the lame man that they did not have what he was hoping for: alms, money. (We could dwell long on their "such as I have," for all of us have *something* to give, whatever the need.)

A look, a command "in the Name of Jesus Christ of Nazareth", an outstretched helping hand—and the man who had never walked in his life stood and walked and leaped. We can imagine his trying out all the things he had seen other people do during the long years he had lain helpless by the temple.

By what power had this miracle been accomplished? Peter and John were to be called into account. And it is worth noting that their critics added, "Or by what name, have ye done this?" They recognized that there was power in the name of Jesus of Nazareth, even while they would not accept Him as Messiah, as Saviour.

How often in times of temptation, of stress and distress, of sickness and pain, do we call on God for His help, praying in the name of Jesus!

People around us, themselves seemingly unbelievers, are aware of this power that is ours as Christians. I have a very dear neighbor who brings her troubles to me, for as she puts it, *"God hears your prayers."* I know He does, for I pray "in Jesus' name." And you can, too.

BUT YOU DO NOT KNOW MY NEIGHBOR

BIBLE READING: Ephesians 4:21-27

Don't sin by nursing your grudge (v. 26, TLB).

"That neighbor of mine! She makes me so *mad*," a Christian woman complained," and it doesn't help any when I read in the Bible that I'm not supposed to ever get angry."

"*Is* that what the Bible says?" responded the friend to whom the gripe was being made. "I read in my Bible, 'Be angry and sin not' and there's quite a difference."

"But you don't know my neighbor" was the retort. And maybe you and I have said or thought the same about some neighbor.

God knew who our neighbors would be; He knew the provocation they would cause us—and us them. But the scriptural injunction is still, "Be ye angry and sin not." *The Living Bible* paraphrases it, "If you are angry, don't sin by nursing your grudge."

The next part of the verse is equally significant and distinctly related to the first: "Don't let the sun go down with you still angry—get over it quickly."

When we don't do this, when we "nurse our grudge," not only do we fracture our relationships with our neighbors but also we make ourselves miserable. And as the Scripture makes so abundantly clear, "You give a mighty foothold to the devil." Having snared us into becoming angry and then encouraging us to do nothing to make amends for what we have done, Satan has us in a bind. It will also cause us to feel guilty, and that will engender more anger (at ourselves), and Satan can have a field day with our emotions and with our testimony.

We need to recognize that we have this potential for

becoming angry and then pray sincerely, daily, for grace to overcome anger. When we fail, we do have recourse with God (1 John 1:9) and with one another. We *can* have a good relationship, even with that neighbor who formerly "made us so mad."

With everything straightened out before nightfall, we can face the new day without a backlog of anger and bitterness of spirit.

THE ON-GOING DEBT

BIBLE READING: Romans 13:7-11

I am debtor (Romans 1:14).

Some people pride themselves on never owing anyone anything. "I pay my debts," they are frequently heard to say. This is, of course, commendable, especially in an era when financial indebtedness is on a runaway course. But, does "debt" always refer to money?

We know it does not. One neighbor borrows from another, usually some household commodity. Some promptly repay. Others are the bane of their neighbor's life because they rarely pay back what they borrow.

I wonder how we make God feel by our frequent neglect to pay what we owe spiritually, for like Paul we, too, are debtors. We owe it to those who are a part of our daily lives to share the Gospel with them. How much do we owe?

"Owe no man anything but to love one another," Paul urges, thereby inferring that love is an on-going debt. We never pay the final installment. Knowing this, we should be conscious of our responsibility to meet our payments. We should be on the lookout for ways to demonstrate Christian love to our neighbors. This is the essence of keeping the Ten Commandments. "All ten are wrapped up in this one"

(v. 9, TLB); then Paul goes on to say, "Love works no ill to his neighbor." That makes sense. If we love our neighbor as much as we love ourselves, we will not break a commandment.

Paul rarely misses a chance to remind us that time is running out for all of us, that what we would do, we should be doing now. If we are going to reduce our debt to mankind, we are going to have to be working at it. Perhaps it would be good to check on ourselves each night by asking, "Have I discharged part of my debt today? Have I told one person that Jesus loves her?"

FROM A POSITION OF CHOICE

BIBLE READING: Romans 12:14-19

Never pay back evil for evil (v. 17, TLB).

A couple of women had spent some time visiting for their church. Some calls had proven worthwhile, but at other homes they had been treated coldly and with some unfriendliness. As the afternoon wore on, the younger woman commented about the other's attitude and behavior.

"You keep so calm, and you speak so nicely to everyone, no matter what kind of a reception we get," she said.

"That's no more than I should do," the other replied, "and besides, why should I let someone else determine how I'm going to act?"

We don't have to repay evil with evil.

We can use our God-given minds and the freedom of choice with which God has endowed us to decide how we will act and react.

On a recent Sunday I learned of a beautiful instance of "heaping coals of fire" on another person's head. A little first-grader arrived at Sunday school with a badly bruised face and a black eye. Her teacher naturally asked the little girl what had happened. The pupil explained that a neighbor boy had been throwing stones in his backyard and that one had hit her in the face.

"What happened to the boy?" the teacher inquired. And with the sweetest smile on her disfigured face (I saw this part myself), the little girl said, "Nothing happened to him. I invited him to Sunday school with me. There he is!" and she pointed to the boy, in Sunday school for the first time.

The little girl and her parents had chosen not to "avenge themselves." They had chosen to "bless her persecutor."

When we operate from this position of choice, when we exercise our free will, we are generally much happier persons.

It is a never-failing spiritual principle the apostle Paul is spelling out for us here. God does not need us to help Him judge people and decree their punishment. Also, Jesus distinctly said, "Judge not, that ye be not judged (Matthew 7:1). As mature believers we can content ourselves with returning *good* for evil, having deliberately chosen to do so.

BREAKING THE GENERATION CYCLE

BIBLE READING: Jeremiah 31:1-3

Jesus Christ, the same yesterday, and today, and forever (Hebrews 13:8).

Two neighbors were chatting over their midmorning coffee, while their toddlers played around. The younger kept a sharp eye on her little girl and from time to time admonished her "not to touch." After a few such cautions, the mother called the child to her, stood her at her knee, and most solemnly said, "Mommie doesn't love you when you're naughty," emphasizing each word with her index finger.

This pattern was repeated a number of times in the course of the coffee break. Finally, the other woman, in whose home the incident was taking place, said kindly, "Would you mind if I say something?"

"Go ahead," the young mother said, "what is it?"

"I hope you'll understand," the other began, "I used to do the same thing myself, until I learned better—I mean, I used to tell my little girl I didn't love her when she was naughty."

"Why—what's wrong with that?" Surprise made the mother's eyes grow large. "She has to learn," she defended herself, "and who else is going to teach her if I don't? That's what my mother always told me. She didn't love *me* when I was naughty."

"You're right about teaching her. Of course, you must do that. But what I mean is that when you tell a child you don't love her when she does something that displeases you, she has no way of knowing that it's *her behavior* you don't like. You still love *her,* don't you?"

The young mother sat deep in thought, obviously contemplating an entirely new concept. And that was the day the older woman had an opportunity to tell her young neighbor of the God of love, of His love that doesn't change, of love that can keep on loving us even while God disapproves of what we may be doing.

It was a double bonus day for the witnessing Christian. Her young neighbor accepted Christ as her Saviour because the woman had related God's unchanging love to the mother's provisional love for her own child. Not only that, but with new understanding she would no longer make her love for her little girl conditional on the child's behavior. She had broken a generation cycle.

THINGS GO BETTER WITH PRAYER

BIBLE READING: Matthew 6:9-13

Pray ye, therefore (Matthew 9:38).

We are familiar with the saying, "The family that prays together, stays together." It has almost become a Christian cliche, and though it has all the elements of truth, it doesn't always work out in real life. There are families who do pray together who then do not "stay together." One strays from the faith of his fathers; another may develop doubts as to the value of praying; or one of the family members may become openly rebellious.

How, then, can we say that things go better with prayer? For *they do!*

Jesus believed in the power of prayer. Have you thought that with all of His emphasis on "going into all the world to preach the Gospel," the only instruction Christ gave there in Matthew 9 was, "Pray ye, therefore."

What *is* prayer?

A day or so ago, I sat at a luncheon where the conversation turned to the topic of prayer: *how* we pray—that we tend to *ask-ask-ask,* that there is a *dearth of thanksgiving* in our praying, that we *neglect to tell our Lord that we love Him,* and that *the spirit of adoration is missing.*

Of course, this is generalizing; it may not be true of you at all. But what these people were saying is that if things are going to go better with prayer, we will have to be sure we really are praying, not just listing our wants.

Jesus provided us with the elements of true and acceptable prayer. In a brief sixty-six words it encompasses: the *fatherhood* of God (toward believers); *reverence; submission to the will of God; daily provision* for our needs; the vital importance of being *forgiving;* our resources against *temptation;* and finally, an acknowledgement that God *is* God—the King all glorious.

We must not fail to mention another prayer (Luke 18: 13): "God be merciful to me, a sinner." When we have earnestly prayed this prayer and put due emphasis on the Lord's Prayer, we will find that things do "go better."

THE WAITING GAME

BIBLE READING: Romans 5:1-5

I waited patiently for the Lord (Psalm 40:1).

I wonder how many Christians can honestly join David in saying, "I waited patiently." Waited—yes. *Patiently*—that may be open to question (or am I the only impatient foot-tapping one among us?).

Paul appears to have gone one step beyond David in this matter of being patient. He gloried in the trials that produced patience in himself.

What was the clue to their ability to display patience, to "play the waiting game" without becoming frustrated? *Hope.* An attitude of hopefulness was their secret. Someone has defined patience as "hope spun out." This is the patience of the farmer and the gardener. They can be patient during the long weeks or months that elapse between sowing and harvesting because they planted in hope.

Sometimes we become impatient with God. We pray for something, and if we are honest about our feelings, we add, "and, Lord, I want it now." But as a wise minister counsels his parishioners, "God answers us in one of three ways: "Yes," "No," and "Wait a while." When the answer does not come speedily enough for us, we may in our immaturity want to "dig up our prayer to see if it's beginning to sprout." Meanwhile, if we could only see and understand, God is moving in the circumstances to make "all things work together for good." Looking back, we can often see that it was best that we had to wait.

In addition to hope, we can see, then, that patience calls for *faith*. This is especially true when, as Paul learned, patience comes by way of tribulation. The trials themselves are never desirable, but when they are God's messengers to teach us to trust Him more, to have faith in Him, to have patience, then like Paul, we can glory in them. There's always a happy "afterwards" for the Christian who accepts what God sends her way. It pays to wait patiently on the Lord.

In an impatient age, people around us need to see patience exhibited.

WE CAN KNOW WE ARE RIGHT
WITH GOD

BIBLE READING: 1 John 3:18-24

If our heart condemn us not (v. 21).

Some people would have us believe that it's presumptuous for us to feel that we have a clear channel of communication with God. But according to the apostle John, we *can* know and feel this "right" relationship in the same way we can know we are at peace with a friend or a neighbor.

What creates this confidence? Verse 21 gives us the answer. Also, in chapter 5 the thought is amplified: "This is the confidence that we have in him, that, if we ask anything according to his will, he heareth us; and . . . we have the petitions that we desired of him" (vv. 14-15).

So there are certain steps we can take to assure ourselves, to guarantee that our heart will condemn us not:

1. *We seek the will of God.* We can be certain the will

of God will never be contrary to the Word of God, so this is a sure criterion.

2. *We obey the will of God* as He reveals it to us in answer to our prayer and searching of the Scriptures. The result is spelled out very plainly: "We receive, . . . because we keep his commandments, and do those things that are pleasing in his sight."

3. *We "abide in Him."* This has the connotation of constant communication, not just running to God in an emergency but keeping in tune with Him hourly, daily.

Such thinking should be easy for us to grasp. As children when we knew we were doing what our parents wanted us to do, when we were pleasing them, we never hesitated to run and ask for something. "This was the confidence we had"; "Our heart condemned us not."

We need to keep in mind that this theme has nothing whatever to do with our *salvation.* We could *never* summon up enough worth in ourselves for that! But beyond conversion there is the exciting world of living for Christ, of knowing the joy of clear-channel communication. Nothing on earth will ever give us the peace that comes from having a heart that condemns us not.

JUST THREE LITTLE WORDS

BIBLE READING: Galatians 5:19-25

And don't make plans to enjoy evil (Romans 13: 14, TLB).

As Christians we tend to sluff off "the works of the flesh" when we read this chapter. Perhaps we rationalize, "I don't belong in any of these categories; I'm no adulterer, idolator, or murderer; nor am I an habitual liar or a person who would steal from her neighbor. Oh, maybe I'm a bit envious at times, even a little hateful, but—" Then we move on to the "good part," the fruit of the Spirit.

But—not so fast! What about the little phrase at the end of the list of "works"? The Holy Spirit does not use words idly. The three little words, "and such like" could have been omitted unless they had a purpose. What is their purpose? I believe it is to cause us to stop to examine ourselves. Evaluate, "What 'such like' in my life is displeasing to the Lord and cannot be listed in the fruit of the Spirit?"

You will have to judge your "such likes"; and I, mine.

As I pondered this portion of Scripture one day, the Lord showed me my tendency toward a critical spirit. I confessed to this "such like," and with a new awareness, I continually ask the Lord to keep me from being critical of other people. I'm a happier person since that day, for we cannot have negative feelings toward other people and feel good about ourselves.

It's good to do some spiritual house-cleaning.

One thing we have to guard against, however, is just dragging all the works of the flesh (including the "such likes") out of the drawers, cupboards, and closets of our life, shaking our head over some of the ones we know we should discard, and then—unable to part with them—stuffing them all back where they were before, shutting the drawers and doors!

Rather, we need to be ruthless. Toss them out. Give them no room. As *The Living Bible* puts it, "Ask the Lord Jesus Christ to help you live as you should, and don't make plans to enjoy evil." Then make provision for the fruit of the Spirit.

LEARNING FROM THE MASTER

BIBLE READING: John 3:9-17

How can these things be? (v. 9).

Among the priceless lessons of John 3 is the glimpse into the methods our Lord used in dealing with individuals. (John 4 offers another example.)

How can we apply these timeless lessons in our own situation?

A neighbor comes for a little visit; and in the course of the conversation, she asks a direct question such as, "What does your church believe?" or, "Do you think there's a hell?" With Christ as your teacher, you will draw her out rather than submitting a ready answer that could conclude the discussion.

The initial question is, many times, really a bid for you to share your faith. By looking interested and saying something like, "I'm glad you asked that," or "That's a very good question," you make the person feel she has posed a question that is both intelligent and worthy of discussion.

It's wise never to over-answer (sometimes known as "scratching a person where she doesn't itch"). Rather, by exploring the neighbor's own question, you can help her to sort out her own thinking on the subject. This is always wiser than launching into some deep dissertation of Bible truth with one who has just shown a mild interest and who may not have a clue as to what Christianity is all about.

Jesus is the only One who can speak to a person from His position of total knowledge of the person. He, the master Soul-winner, dealt with Nicodemus on the basis of what Nicodemus himself knew, using figures of speech which were familiar to the religious leader.

It's good, too, to steer away from "Christianese," phrases commonly used by evangelical Christians but which have no meaning for the non-Christian. (I vividly recall my own bewilderment over "the leeks and garlic of Egypt" when I was a brand new Christian with virtually no Bible background.)

As you take this neighbor where she is, not giving a too-ready answer but showing a great deal of interest in her questions, it may be that God will give you the privilege of answering when she asks the million-dollar question, "What must I do to be saved?"

SPECIAL ASSIGNMENT

BIBLE READING: Acts 9:10-18

He is praying to me right now (v. 11, TLB).

A Christian felt a strong urge to visit a neighbor whom she had not talked with for some weeks because their paths had not crossed during that time. She couldn't think of any particular reason to go that morning, but neither could she shake the feeling that she should go.

She finally walked the short distance and was met by the neighbor with looks of utter astonishment. The woman's face showed traces of recent tears. "Come in," she urged, still shaking her head in unbelief. "What made you come this morning? I've been up most of the night, and I've been praying for hours that God would send someone to help me." And she began to pour out her troubles.

What if the Christian neighbor had disregarded the prompting of the Spirit?

What if Ananias had refused to obey the voice of the Lord? But he didn't. He must have felt he was putting his neck in a noose; nevertheless, after a little demurring, "Ananias went." Not only so, he went the other mile. He *accepted* Saul the notorious terror of the Christians. He called him *"Brother* Saul." Imagine being the very first person to encourage the apostle Paul!

111

(Someone has written, "Hell will be knowing what we *could* have been, what we *could* have done.")

God still chooses people for special assignments. His doing so depends on our believing that He does and our believing that He will choose you and me. And we can be confident that He will never send us to be the answer to a person's prayer without providing us with the answer.

What does it mean to the one to whom we are sent? First, it says that God heard her prayer and that He did not place it in a "future" file or table the request. Then, too, it tells the person that God cared enough to send someone to answer the prayer, and third, it shows that a Christian cared enough to listen to God, to heed, and to obey.

Maybe God has a special assignment for you today, to answer a neighbor's prayer.

WE ARE NOT ORPHANS

BIBLE READING: Ephesians 1:1-5

His unchanging plan has always been to adopt us (v. 5, TLB).

Lecturing on the legal aspects of adoption, a professor told his class that unlike a natural child born into the family, an adopted child could never be disinherited. Think of the implications this fact has for the Christian!

You have probably heard some adoptive parent say to her adopted child when the child had been taunted by other children, "Tell them that we *chose* you to be our little boy because we loved you and we wanted you." This same reinforcement is ours when we might feel tempted to doubt God's loving care, when some people might say to us, "Where *is* God? He must have forgotten all about you."

God never forgets all about us. His Word tells us that clearly and plainly: "I will never leave you nor forsake you" (Hebrews 13:5), and "Like as a father pitieth his children, so the Lord pitieth them that fear Him. For He knoweth our frame" (Psalm 103:13-14*a*).

We will never be "orphans," for God will never disown or disinherit us.

Why, then, do we sometimes act as though we are fatherless?

When we fret and worry, showing undue concern both for the present and the future, we are, in a sense, saying to people around us (and to ourselves) that either God has forgotten us, or if He still remembers us, He doesn't *care* any more. Then what happens?

We lose the blessing that can be ours by "simply trusting every day." And not only do we rob ourselves, we rob our neighbors who may be observing and taking us as a pattern of Christianity.

Recently someone shared with me a note that accompanied her salary check. The note from the company treasurer, who knew the severe trials this woman was going through, read, "You continue to amaze me by such a continually wonderful spirit."

Under stress, she had shown that she was not an "orphan." You and I can, too.

CHRIST HAS NO PLAN "B"

BIBLE READING: Luke 24:44-51

Ye shall be witnesses (Acts 1:8).

It's just an allegory, but it speaks to believers in every generation. The scene is heaven. The time is Ascension Day, A.D. 30.*

After a time of worship and rejoicing, the angel Gabriel

*Berkeley Version in Modern English, N.T.: 121 fn. *a*.*

asks the Lord Jesus what plans He has made for the gospel to be carried to the whole world.

"I have left my band of disciples and the five hundred who believe. They will proclaim the message," Jesus answers.

"What if they fail?" the angel questions. "If they do *not* tell the lost world—what other plan do You have, Lord?"

And Jesus replies, "I have no other plan."

Was Christ's complete trust in His followers a potent factor in their faithfulness to the charge He left them? *"Ye shall be witnesses* unto me." These were His parting words on that Ascension Day. Witnesses at home and abroad. Empowered by the Holy Spirit as Jesus promised they would be, they became the dauntless evangels who "counted not their lives dear," many of them witnessing unto the death.

Jesus had no "Plan B"; He believed implicitly that He was leaving behind Him men and women who, through the power of the indwelling Spirit, could turn the world upside down. And they did! Never was so much accomplished by so few, with so little resources for evangelism.

God's "Plan A" is still the only hope of lost men and women, boys and girls—among them some of our own neighbors.

The Lord Jesus bids us love our neighbor. This is the ultimate in loving: seeking to win our neighbor to Christ, sharing Christ's offer of sins forgiven, peace with God, and the sure hope of Heaven that we ourselves enjoy. Like the disciples we, too, are entrusted with this tremendous assignment from our Lord. We need to activate His Plan A; it is still operative. Christ has no Plan B.

HOW BIG IS YOUR GOD?

BIBLE READING: Isaiah 40:12-18

How can we describe God? With whom can we compare Him? (v. 18, TLB).

Waiting for a traffic light to change, I was confronted with a bumper sticker on the car ahead of me. "How big is YOUR God?" it asked me, and I found myself caught up in the provocative question.

How big is my God, your God? As big as we will let Him be in our lives! This was the only conclusion that satisfied me.

Isaiah had no problem with how big or how great and majestic our God is: "All the peoples of the world are nothing in comparison with Him—they are but a drop in the bucket, dust on the scales" (v. 15, TLB).

As Isaiah wrote later, "I dwell in the high and holy place, with him also that is of a contrite and humble spirit" (57: 15).

That's how big God is!

The Lord will not force Himself upon us, however. He has given us freedom of choice, and He will never violate His own design by living in our hearts unless we ask Him to. God wants to be "big" in our lives *for our good.* But it will be at our request, as we say "Take my life and let it be consecrated unto Thee."

When we really want God to be big in our lives, we will be reasoning like John the Baptist when he said of the Lord Jesus Christ, "He must increase, but I must decrease" (John 3:30). We must decrease in self-importance, letting God make us important.

And the wonderful part is that no matter how we have failed in the past, we can come to the Lord today and pray, "I want You to be big in my life today, Father." There is no road back to yesterday so it's futile to mope and beat ourselves over the head over something which we cannot undo. All we have to do is to confess that we have been stubbornly trying to go it alone and that it has not worked; we have been personally frustrated and fruitless in our efforts to win our neighbors to the Lord. But that's in the past. Now we know how big our God is.

LIFE WITH A CAPITAL "L"

BIBLE READING: Genesis 2:1-8

And the Lord God, . . . breathed into his nostrils the breath of life (v. 7).

Asked the secret of his success, Mark Twain answered, "I was born *excited*."

Of all people we Christians should be the most excited about living.

Who among us was not exhilarated when we were born again!

God Himself breathed life into the first man.

God the Holy Spirit indwelt us at our second birth. Isn't that something to get excited about? To remain excited about? Nothing is more contagious than the enthusiasm of a new convert. But why should there be some unwritten law that time should "cure" this Christian excitement over what Christ has done for us?

A Christian woman, obviously embarrassed at a man's enthusiastic singing in church, whispered to his wife nearby, "Can't you get Harry to tone down a bit?" And the incredible part of this is that she had prayed for years that Harry would be saved.

The enthusiasm to which I refer is not some kind of pumped-up froth that will fizzle out like a pricked balloon when some adversity strikes. The true, Spirit-born excitement will prevail and will buoy us up even when the ill winds are blowing our way. This enthusiasm is an elixir of life, something which my Scottish countrymen would say "is better felt than telt [told]." If it is to last, this spiritual excitement must be fed from its original source. The Holy Spirit, who engendered it, will maintain it at the same magnetic level as we read God's Word, obey it, and commune often with Him. It's not God's will that we should be yo-yo Christians, one day up and the next day *under* the circumstances."

God has made us all different—some effervescent and some phlegmatic. But for each of us, the Christian life is life with a capital *L*. It would be hard to have the life of Christ in us and *not* be excited.

YOU CAN'T BUY IT BACK

BIBLE READING: Proverbs 22:1-11

To be held in loving esteem is better than silver and gold (v. 1, TLB).

At the unveiling of a statue of the late Sir Winston Churchill, Queen Elizabeth said, "I offered Sir Winston a dukedom . . . but such a man needs no higher honor or recognition than the name 'Winston Churchill.'"

A good name is priceless, and it takes time to build, for as L. Pearsall Smith has written, "Our names are labels plainly printed on the bottled essence of our past behavior." But we cannot rest on our past behavior. It's Satan's business to try to trap the Christian into falling; not only can he then blacken the believer's reputation, he can cause the name of Christ to be blasphemed.

We guard what we consider valuable in this life. But I wonder if we always "take heed lest we fall" (1 Corinthians 10:12). One's reputation, once sullied is almost impossible to redeem. There's not enough gold in Fort Knox to buy it back. Oh, God forgives and forgets, but men and women do not always forgive or forget.

It's important to the testimony of all Christians that we do not fall into sin. How often, for example, have you been stymied in your attempt to witness to a neighbor by her saying, "Don't talk to me about God and the church and religion. I know so-and-so. She used to talk like you, but look at her now!" Because of another believer's actions, the cause of Christ is hurt.

Not only for the sake of our testimony is this vital, however. Our own emotional welfare is at stake, for we have to live with *ourselves* first. And the person who has lost his or her reputation, her good name, lives a haunted life.

In our own strength we would fail against the wiles of our enemy. But God is our strength and shield. By keeping close to Him, we can guard against falling, against throwing away our good name that we can never buy back.

HOW TO BE MORE THAN A NUMBER

BIBLE READING: Isaiah 45:1-5

He calleth his own sheep by name (John 10:3).

Have you noticed that certain business places, notably banks, are training their staffs to use the customer's name? We like this, for we interpret it as their showing a personal interest in us, not treating us like the numbers on our account. Moreover, it's heartening in this day when people are feeling, "I'm just a number, a set of punch marks on a computer card."

A recent film documentary, shown at the 1973 Evangelical Press Association Convention, portrayed all of humanity as a completely computerized society. At birth a child was given a number which would be his identifying code from the cradle to the grave and which would permit him to be located in a matter of seconds no matter where on Planet Earth he might be. "It's totally dehumanizing," said the narrator, Walter Cronkite, "and we are fast moving in that direction." He went on to hypothesize that this was a major cause of the sickness in our world today.

Making a person into a mere number robs him of the dignity with which God endowed mankind.

Isn't it encouraging and heart-warming, then, to realize that, as Christians, you and I are not digits to be programmed into a computer but persons—individuals—*whom the Lord knows by name.*

Did you ever try to communicate with a computer?

Jesus not only calls us by name, He leads us. And because we recognize His voice, we follow Him. We know His voice. He knows our name. There's a world of warmth and love and caring in Christ's concern for His own.

Next time your neighbor is justifiably griping about "being nothing but a number," wouldn't it be good to let her in on your secret of how to be more than a number?

Everybody longs to be important enough that her name is known to somebody. We can all have the assurance that *God* knows our names and that Jesus calls us by our names.

TRY ANOTHER APPROACH

BIBLE READING: Proverbs 15:1-7

He that is slow to wrath is of great understanding (Proverbs 14:29).

Sometimes our most earnest efforts to win a neighbor to the Lord bring no success. A different approach may then be indicated. For example, Amy and her friend, Grace, had covenanted with one another to try to lead one neighbor each to the Lord in a given time. They met one morning in the supermarket, and Grace asked, "How are you making out with our project?"

"I keep trying," Anne said, "but my neighbor gets so angry! What can I do about it? I don't want to give up on her."

Anne's persistence is commendable. She's wise also in realizing that her approach is not working. Psychologists are agreed that, when a person is angry and hostile, he is not listening to what another person is saying. He's engrossed with his angry feelings.

What can we do in such a situation? There are a number of possibilities, and of course, different people respond to different approaches. It's helpful if you can remember how you, yourself, felt the first time someone witnessed to you, telling you of your need to accept Christ as your Saviour. Were *you* angry? Then you can say to the neighbor who is angry, "I think I know how you feel; something I just said has made you a little upset. Maybe we could talk about it?"

Normally, this accomplishes two things. First, it makes your neighbor feel you are on her side, not standing off to one side judging her. (She may have been viewing your honest efforts for her own good as "judging or condemning her.") Second, by your building a better relationship with her, you open a wider door for your witnessing. The fact that you do not react with anger when she is angry is also a powerful influence.

We can be sure that, when God lays a particular person on our hearts, He will give us the needed insight concerning the best approach for winning that person to Himself. Perhaps we should pray not only, "Lord, help me win my neighbor," but also, "Lord, *show me how best to do it.*" And He will!

MAJORING ON THEIR STRENGTHS

BIBLE READING: Ecclesiastes 3:1-7

A time to keep silence, and a time to speak (v. 7).

It was time for the neighborhood get-together, and one of the group had not yet arrived.

"It won't bother me if Phyllis doesn't show up at all," one of the women remarked. "She's so opinionated." This was all it took for the others to mention what they didn't like about their absent neighbor. It might have continued except for the fact that one person cut in with, "She might be all the things you're saying about her, but you have to admit that she does get things done. And besides, all the kids in the neighborhood like her."

By speaking up at the right time, this one woman changed the whole tenor of the conversation. The others nodded, agreeing that, yes, there was something about Phyllis that attracted their own children and others. In talking about this they found a number of good qualities in her so that when a few minutes later she breezed in, all apologies for being late, they were able to say, "Too bad! You missed all the nice things we were saying about you."

When we can major on a person's strengths, we keep from dwelling on her weak points. This is one way we can help "cover a multitude of sins" in one another.

In dealing with young people, we must not major on their failings or weaknesses. For instance, take the neighbor boy who cuts your lawn or does odd jobs for a little cash in his pocket. Do you sometimes find yourself saying after inspecting his work, "But *as usual,* you forgot to put the lid on the garbage can" or some deflating complaint? Not only does this damage the boy's own self-image, it also causes him to dislike you, and any good influence you might have upon him is destroyed.

Sometimes people are like porcupines: they seem to exhibit only their bad points. You may have to work to find something positive to say. When you find it, that's the time to speak. The time to be silent is when speaking would put someone else in a bad light.

WHERE WILL YOU FIND A BETTER OFFER?

BIBLE READING: Psalm 84

Delight thyself . . . in the Lord; and he shall give thee the desires of thine heart (Psalm 37:4)

In a rather petulant voice a Christian complained to her pastor, "Other people get their prayers answered. I don't see why God doesn't answer *mine.*"

You may have felt like this sometimes.

We can't determine for each other why God does or does not answer a particular prayer. But the Bible is explicit on the subject: "No good thing will he withhold from them that walk uprightly."

Think of the implications of this offer! No "fine print," no time limit.

There is one *condition,* however. The offer is for those who "walk uprightly." Now we do not have to quibble concerning God's meaning. As Christians we have a conscience about such things. We have God's Word to guide us; we have the indwelling Holy Spirit to tell us when we are "upright" and to convict us when we are not. Oh, we will stumble, we may fall at times, in our Christian walk. But the Lord knows our hearts. If we are earnest about our intent, He will help us up when we falter and fall.

To further assure us, we have the promise, "Delight thyself in the Lord and He will give thee the desires of thine heart." What better guarantee can we request? We see this principle at work in the parent/child relationship. A father or mother says, "My children are such a delight to me that there's nothing I wouldn't do for them." But we are limited by what we *can* do: not so the Lord. No shortage can limit our fathomless God. He supplies our needs "according to his riches in glory by Christ Jesus" (Philippians 4:19).

Wouldn't this be a good day to question ourselves, "Am I delighting myself in the Lord? Am I endeavoring to walk uprightly before Him? Is my heart right with God?"

Having settled this vital matter, we can ask God for some "good thing"—and expect to receive it.

BUT MY NEIGHBOR'S IN A *CULT*

BIBLE READING: 1 John 4:1-6

He that hath the Son hath life (1 John 5:12).

If the gospel were a jigsaw puzzle, no one but a true Christian could put it all together, for only a born-again believer would have the "piece" to fit the shape of eternal life.

So your neighbor is an ardent member of a cult! Then she has no assurance of eternal life. She has a God-shaped vacuum in her life.

But it's so hard to reach the person who is steeped in a cultist doctrine, too many of us are prone to think. A few days ago I heard a convert say, "I came to know Jesus Christ as my personal Saviour through the witness of some young people who didn't *know* a Jehovah's witness was too hard to reach."

From his own experience Professor Edmund Gruss of Los Angeles Baptist College urges Christians to give the cultists a chance to hear the truth. "Tell them about Christ's offer of eternal life through faith in His Blood shed on the

Cross," he suggests. "They are all working for their salvation, not realizing that 'He that heareth my Word and believeth on him that sent me, hath everlasting life' (John 5:24)."*

What is believing? It is trusting what God says in His Word, turning our case over to Jesus Christ for Him to handle, acknowledging that it is "not by works of righteousness which we have done, but according to his mercy He saves us" (Titus 3:5). We know this, but what of our cultist neighbor?

Suppose, seeing us in our sin and unbelief, Christians had decided we were "hard to reach" and content in our own religion, and left us unreached?

Every person who ever lived has the same inner, basic needs. Only Christ can fill them. Everybody wants ultimately to reach heaven. We know *the* Way. Our cultist neighbor knows only *a* way "and the end thereof are the ways of death" (Proverbs 14:12). Are we going to be intimidated, or will we reach out to this needy neighbor with the Gospel, thereby being the finest of "good neighbors."

EVERY DAY IS THANKSGIVING

BIBLE READING: Psalm 89:1-8

Blessed be the Lord who daily loadeth us with benefits (Psalm 68:19).

Did you ever read a verse so saturated with praise and appreciation and joyful acknowledgement of the goodness of God? No wonder the psalmist could exclaim, "I will sing of the mercies of the LORD for ever."

---

*From a sermon preached in Trinity Baptist Church, November 1973. Used by permission.

Loads of blessings! That's better than one-a-day vitamins any day!

But what are some of these benefits which God showers upon us? Suppose your neighbor was to overhear you singing the praises of God for His mercies to you, and she asked, "Okay, tell me about just *one*." What would you say? Would a whole host of things come to your mind and tumble over each other as you shared them with your inquiring neighbor, or would you have to scratch your head, screw up your face in deep thought, and perhaps say, "Oh, you caught me unawares with that question. Let me think for a minute."

You and I may look differently upon some "mercies," but there is one we are sure to be agreed upon: our *salvation*. And the God who daily loads us with benefits is "the God of our salvation." It's important to keep this in mind. We will always be ready, then, to answer the person who asks us for what we are thankful.

"It is a good thing to give thanks unto the LORD," the Bible tells us (Psalm 92:1). It's also a healthy thing: it's emotionally healthy. For when we are being thankful for specific blessings, our minds are dwelling on these good things; this keeps us from morose and gloom-producing preoccupation with things we do not consider blessings.

A thankful spirit has to be cultivated. We're not born thankful. Rather, we come into the world grasping little mortals who feel the world owes us everything. And some children because they have never been taught the grace of being thankful, grow up expecting the world owes them a living. As God's children, we can look forward to the time when we will "sing of the mercies of the LORD forever." In the meantime, we can daily thank Him for His daily blessings.

WHEN YOUR NEIGHBOR IS AN IN-LAW

BIBLE READING: 1 John 4:10-21

If God so loved us, we ought also to love one another (v. 11).

Pondering the subject of neighbors one day, I was struck with the fact that the very first neighbors in all the world were relatives of one another. At that time, the commandment "Love thy neighbor" had not yet been issued by God; so these first neighbors were not responsible to obey it.

But it has been given now. And we are responsible to love our neighbor.

How do we treat a neighbor who is also a relative, an in-law possibly?

Can people observing us from day to day note by our behavior and attitudes that we genuinely love each other?

It's so possible for a Christian to be a good neighbor to other people, to be sincere and conscientious about it and yet not see the importance of extending at least the same warmth and love and friendliness to her own relatives.

An old adage is that "the light that shines the farthest, shines the brightest at home." It's delightful and true.

I know of a little girl who brags in her Sunday school class, "Mrs. Brown is *our* teacher—but she's just *my* auntie." And there's a world of love and trust in the child's voice. She feels special because this relative treats her lovingly. (What if this teacher had neglected being a "good neighbor" to the little girl who, though she lived next door and was literally a neighbor, was also a relative. Of how much value would her Sunday school teaching have been to the child, then and in the future when she recalled her teacher?)

Neighbors are an assorted lot; and because they are, some of them may be our relatives, our in-laws on occasion. To the same degree that we will have to give an account of how we have treated other neighbors, God will require an account as to how we have loved our "family" neighbors. "This commandment have we, . . . That he who loveth God love his brother also" (1 John 4:21).

Moody Press, a ministry of the Moody Bible Institute, is designed for education, evangelization and edification. If we may assist you in knowing more about Christ and the Christian life, please write us without obligation to: Moody Press, c/o MLM, Chicago, Illinois 60610.